Let us know what you think!

Did the information in this book resonate with you? We're hoping you'll continue to support this book's journey to reaching teachers and having the ultimate impact in the classroom. Here are a few ways you can do that:

> > > **JOIN** the conversation! Share your comments, participate in an online book study, or post a picture of yourself with the book on social media using #CorwinMath.

> > > **PROVIDE** your expert review of *Figuring Out Fluency—Addition and Subtraction With Whole Numbers: A Classroom Companion* on Amazon or Goodreads.

> > > **LEAD** or join a book study in your school or team to share ideas on how to bring the concepts presented in the book to life.

> > > **FOLLOW** our Corwin Facebook page and share your experiences figuring out fluency using #CorwinMath.

> > > **RECOMMEND** this book for your Professional Learning Community activities.

> > > **SUGGEST** this book to teacher educators.

Be sure to stay up-to-date on all things Corwin by following us on social media:
Facebook: www.facebook.com/CorwinPress
Instagram: www.instagram.com/corwin_press, @corwin_press
Twitter: twitter.com/CorwinPress, @CorwinPress
Pinterest: www.pinterest.com/corwinpress/pins

www.corwin.com

"This text provides a clear definition of what fluency really is and provides strategies to deepen students' number sense and make them fluent mathematicians."

Meghan Schofield
Third-Grade Teacher

"I wish I'd had this book when I was in the classroom 10 years ago. The authors clearly lay out a pathway to procedural fluency, including intentional activities to understand and practice specific strategies, while also advocating for space for students to make decisions and feel empowered as mathematical thinkers and doers."

Kristine M. Gettelman
Instructional Designer
CenterPoint Education

"This book is a must-read for teachers wanting to learn more about focused math fluency instruction. The steps are clear and easy to follow. You will have all the steps to help your students become fluent math thinkers."

Carly Morales
Instructional Coach
District 93

"Are you ready to help your students connect their Number Talks and number routines to the real world? *Figuring Out Fluency* will give you the routines, games, protocols, and resources you need to help your students build their fluency in number sense (considering reasonableness, strategy selection, flexibility, and more). Our students deserve the opportunity to build a positive and confident mathematics identity. We can help support them to build this identity by providing them with access to a variety of strategies and the confidence to know when to use them."

Sarah Gat
Instructional Coach
Upper Grand District School Board

"*Figuring Out Fluency* goes beyond other resources currently on the market. It not only provides a robust collection of strategies and routines for developing fluency but also pays critical attention to the ways teachers can empower each and every student as a mathematical thinker who can make strategic decisions about their computation approaches. If you are looking for instruction and assessment approaches for fluency that move beyond getting the right answer, this is the resource for you."

Nicole Rigelman
Professor of Mathematics Education
Portland State University

"This book should be on every teacher's desk as a tool for building fluency. Many times, I teach a strategy and wonder why my students go back to a slower, less useful strategy. This book answers that question for me. The games give students a fun and engaging way to use a practice strategy. I can easily differentiate any game for a variety of learners."

Barb Klein
Third-Grade teacher

"*Figuring Out Fluency* provides a wealth of insightful examples and resources to support teachers, students, and parents in learning about and truly understanding computational fluency. As a math coach, I am excited to use this book to plan and teach meaningful lessons with teachers to model efficient strategies for students as they add and subtract."

Marcy Myers
Elementary Mathematics Instructional Leader
Carroll County Public Schools

"Being fluent is much more than solving problems quickly and accurately. This jam-packed resource brings clarity to what it means to be fluent with whole number addition and subtraction and provides numerous ideas for strategy instruction, purposeful practice, and assessment. It's an absolute must-have for everyone who strives to support students in reaching the goal of fluency!!"

Susie Katt
K–2 Mathematics Coordinator
Lincoln Public Schools

"This book is invaluable. SanGiovanni, Bay-Williams, and Serrano don't just provide top tier content for educators, they include strategy briefs for families! I absolutely love the idea of including parents as "partners in the pursuit of fluency.""

Cherelle C. McKnight
Mathematics Specialist, P.O.W.E.R. Academic Strength and Conditioning

"The term *math fluency* may be interpreted in different ways depending on who you ask. This book clearly defines fluency and is a must-have resource for all educators working toward this goal with their students. Each module focuses on different strategies and ways to implement using parent resources, centers, games, and teaching tips. This is the book that you can read and put into immediate action in your classroom."

Cindy Cliche
Murfreesboro City Schools
Math Coordinator

"For years research has indicated that fluency is much more than speed, yet timed assessments and traditional instruction persist for teachers without a clear vision or tools to change their practices. This series provides teachers with the explicit examples, resources, and activities needed to bring that research to life for their students and will quickly become a well-worn guidebook for every fluency-focused classroom. This is the toolkit teachers have been yearning for in their journey toward fluency with their students."

Gina Kilday
Elementary Math Interventionist and MTSS Coordinator

"Fluency isn't a dry landscape of disconnected facts, it is a rich soil for developing and connecting diverse perspectives and ideas. This book series equips you with a deep understanding of fluency and a variety of activities to engage students in co-constructing ideas about addition and subtraction that will last a lifetime."

Berkeley Everett
Math Coach and Facilitator for UCLA Mathematics Project
Math Consultant for DragonBox

"*Figuring Out Fluency* is a must-have, must-read, and must-use for elementary teachers. This text is concise and intentional in communicating the aspects of math fluency and what they look like in action. The routines, tasks, and activities included are easy to implement yet impactful and engaging. Teachers will gain insight for their pedagogy when reading, and students will make strides as problem solvers and flexible thinkers engaging in the activities."

Sumer Smith
Second Grade Teacher

"This book—indeed this *series*—is a must-read for elementary and middle level teachers, coaches, and administrators. Within this resource you will find a synthesis of important research organized to help readers develop a clear and common understanding of fluency paired with a large collection of teaching activities that provide concrete ways to support students' fluency development. *Figuring Out Fluency* provides a much-needed roadmap for teachers looking to increase computational proficiency with multiplication and division."

Delise Andrews
3–5 Mathematics Coordinator Lincoln Public Schools

"The authors John J. SanGiovanni, Jennifer M. Bay-Williams, and Rosalba Serrano shine a bright light on how math fluency is *the* equity issue in mathematics education. How refreshing to have a book that equips math educators with the research and strategies to make a difference for *all* students! Let's implement these strategy modules in this book and help kids figure out fluency once and for all!"

Kelly DeLong
Executive Director for the Kentucky Center for Mathematics
Northern Kentucky University

Figuring Out Fluency—Addition and Subtraction With Whole Numbers: A Classroom Companion
The Book at a Glance

Building off of *Figuring Out Fluency*, this classroom companion dives deep into five of the Seven Significant Strategies that relate to procedural fluency when adding and subtracting whole numbers, beyond basic facts.

FIGURE 12 ● Reasoning Strategies for Adding and Subtracting Whole Numbers

REASONING STRATEGIES	RELEVANT OPERATIONS
1. Count On/Count Back (Module 1)	Addition and Subtraction
2. Make Tens (Module 2)	Addition
3. Partial Sums and Differences (Module 3)	Addition and Subtraction
4. Compensation (Module 4)	Addition and Subtraction
5. Think Addition (Module 5)	Subtraction

Strategy overviews and family briefs communicate how each strategy helps students develop flexibility, efficiency, accuracy, automaticity, and reasonableness.

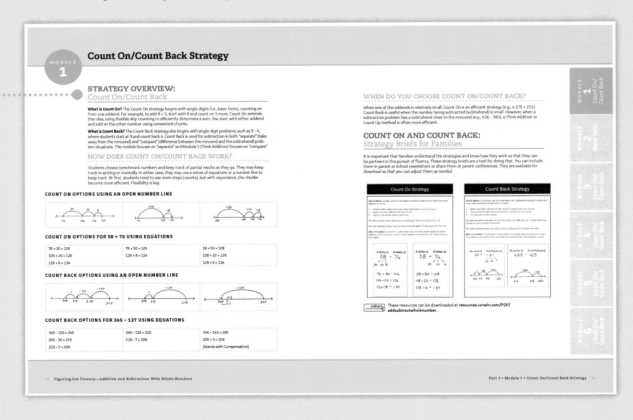

Each strategy module starts with teaching activities that help you explicitly teach the strategy.

TEACHING ACTIVITIES for Count On/ Count Back

Count On and Count Back are often the first strategies students learn. What begins as count on or back by ones becomes count on by tens and then larger chunks like 30 or 100. In this section, you'll find instructional activities for helping students develop efficient ways to count on or count back. The goal is that students become adept at using counting strategies efficiently and accurately and also consider when they will want to use a counting strategy.

ACTIVITY 1.1
CONNECTING REPRESENTATIONS WHEN COUNTING ON

Count On is a strategy for finding the sum when addition is being used. One way to develop this understanding, and to model it, is to represent it with base-10 blocks, place value disks, and number lines. In this activity, have students show Count On with math tools such as place value disks or base-10 blocks. They record adding chunks on a number line or set of equations. The following image shows what this would look like for 132 + 45.

$$132 + 45$$

Students use place value disks to solve the problem.

$$132 + 45$$

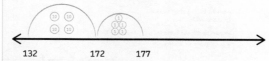

Students later transition to chunking place value disks. They work toward using the least amount of chunks, making it a more efficient strategy.

Each strategy shares worked examples for
you to work through with your students
as they develop their procedural fluency.

2. The student makes an error in breaking apart a number.
- 87 + 71: from 87, counts on 20 to get to 107 and then 40 [rather than 50] to get to 147 and one more to 148.
- 4,225 − 1,270: counts back 1,200 to 3,025, then back 25 to 3,000, then back 55 [rather than 45] to 2,945.

3. The student misses a count when consecutive digits are the same.
- 871 − 449: counts back 4 hundreds to 471 but overlooks 4 tens because a jump of 4 was just made.

Although not an error, students may continue to count by single ones, tens, or hundreds instead of counting in chunks or multiples of these. Show a worked example that does this and ask students to consider how they might combine jumps to add/subtract more efficiently. Various worked examples can be found throughout this module, or you can collect authentic worked examples (see prompts from Activity 1.5, for example). Additionally, have students compare worked examples to highlight different ways to count on or back. A sampling of ideas are provided in the following table.

SAMPLE WORKED EXAMPLES FOR COUNT ON/ COUNT BACK

Correctly Worked Example	Compare Michelle's and Peter's methods for adding 68 + 88:
(make sense of the strategy) What did _____ do? Why does it work? Is this a good method for this problem?	

Partially Worked Example	Nate's start for 546 − 175: $546 - 200 = 346$	Jeannette's start for 546 − 175: $546 - 140 = 406$
(implement the strategy accurately) Why did _____ start the problem this way? What does _____ need to do to finish the problem?		

Incorrectly Worked Example	Luke's work for 705 − 183:
(highlight common errors) What did _____ do? What mistake does _____ make? How can this mistake be fixed?	 Allie's work for 38 + 27:

ACTIVITY 1.6

Name: *"Or You Could?"* **Type:** *Routine*

About the Routine: Count On is most efficient when done in chunks. Students may be comfortable counting on by ones, tens, or hundreds instead of groups. This routine helps students work to use chunks by renaming expressions that add singles as expressions that add groups. In it, students are shown a basic (inefficient) approach to count on or count back. It asks them to think of another way they could carry out the strategy. Keep in mind that it is reasonable for students to first learn and use Count On and Count Back by decomposing a number into individual tens and ones and counting by each. The strategy is most efficiently used by counting on or back by chunks. This routine helps students develop more efficient approaches for counting.

Materials: list of two or three completed examples of Count On or Count Back

Directions: 1. Provide completed Count On or Count Back problems such as the following examples.

· You can solve 26 + 45 by thinking 26 + 10 + 10 + 10 + 10 + 1 + 1 + 1 + 1 + 1 or you could …

· You can solve 92 – 64 by thinking 92 – 10 – 10 – 10 – 10 – 10 – 10 – 1 – 1 – 1 – 1 or you could …

· You can solve 516 + 145 by thinking 516 + 100 + 10 + 10 + 10 + 1 + 1 + 1 + 1 + 1 or you could …

· You could solve 421 – 233 by thinking 400 – 100 – 100 – 10 – 10 – 10 – 1 – 1 – 1 or you could …

2. Ask students to talk with a partner about another way to count on or back.

3. After a few moments, bring the group together to share their thinking.

4. As students share more efficient ways to chunk the skip counts, record their thinking on a number line or with an equation.

5. Reinforce to students how the different approaches yield the same sum or difference.

To note, it's important to avoid using too many approaches. You want students to find and explain efficient approaches. In time, you can begin to modify the routine even further by providing a slightly more efficient chunking as shown in these two examples. Even though the hundreds were chunked, there is still an opportunity to chunk the tens and ones.

● You could solve 716 + 244 by thinking 716 + 200 + 10 + 10 + 10 + 10 + 4 or you could …

● You could solve 91 – 33 by thinking 91 – 1 – 10 – 10 – 10 – 2 or you could …

Keep in mind that sometimes chunking may be manipulated for friendlier computations. For example, in 378 + 344, one might add on 300 (678), then 2 (680), then 20 (700) to make a 10 and then a 100 and last add the remaining 22 (722). No matter how students think about chunking addends or subtrahends for Count On or Count Back, be sure to ask them to explain why that approach is efficient. Also, be sure that you accept their thinking and share other ideas but be careful to avoid saying that one way is "correct."

TEACHING TAKEAWAY
Ask students to explain why an approach is efficient but avoid saying one way is correct.

Routines, Games, and Centers for each strategy offer extensive opportunity for student practice.

Download the resources you need for each activity at this book's companion website.

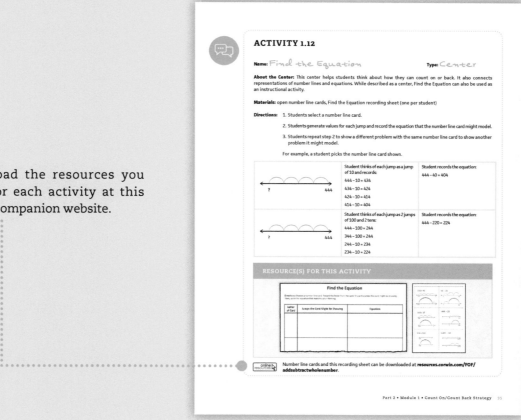

ACTIVITY 1.12

Name: *Find the Equation* **Type:** *Center*

About the Center: This center helps students think about how they can count on or back. It also connects representations of number lines and equations. While described as a center, Find the Equation can also be used as an instructional activity.

Materials: open number line cards, Find the Equation recording sheet (one per student)

Directions: 1. Students select a number line card.

2. Students generate values for each jump and record the equation that the number line card might model.

3. Students repeat step 2 to show a different problem with the same number line card to show another problem it might model.

For example, a student picks the number line card shown.

	Student thinks of each jump as a jump of 10 and records:	Student records the equation:
? 444	444 – 10 = 434 434 – 10 = 424 424 – 10 = 414 414 – 10 = 404	444 – 40 = 404
? 444	Student thinks of each jump as 2 jumps of 100 and 2 tens: 444 – 100 = 344 344 – 100 = 244 244 – 10 = 234 234 – 10 = 224	444 – 220 = 224

RESOURCE(S) FOR THIS ACTIVITY

Number line cards and this recording sheet can be downloaded at **resources.corwin.com/FOF/addsubtractwholenumber**.

FIGURING OUT

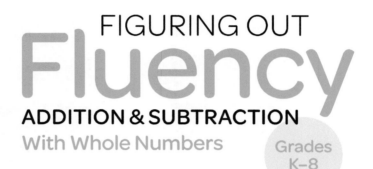

Fluency

ADDITION & SUBTRACTION

With Whole Numbers

Grades
K–8

FIGURING OUT
Fluency
ADDITION & SUBTRACTION
With Whole Numbers

Grades
K–8

A Classroom Companion

John J. SanGiovanni
Jennifer M. Bay-Williams
Rosalba Serrano

CORWIN Mathematics

For information:

Corwin
A SAGE Company
2455 Teller Road
Thousand Oaks, California 91320
(800) 233–9936
www.corwin.com

SAGE Publications Ltd.
1 Oliver's Yard
55 City Road
London, EC1Y 1SP
United Kingdom

SAGE Publications India Pvt. Ltd.
B 1/I 1 Mohan Cooperative
Industrial Area
Mathura Road, New Delhi 110 044
India

SAGE Publications
Asia-Pacific Pte. Ltd.
18 Cross Street #10–10/11/12
China Square Central
Singapore 048423

President: Mike Soules
Associate Vice President and Editorial
   Director: Monica Eckman
Publisher: Erin Null
Content Development Editor:
   Jessica Vidal
Senior Editorial Assistant:
   Caroline Timmings
Production Editor: Tori Mirsadjadi
Copy Editor: Christina West
Typesetter: Integra
Proofreader: Susan Schon
Indexer: Integra
Cover Designer: Rose Storey
Marketing Manager:
   Margaret O'Connor

Printed and bound by CPI Group (UK) Ltd, Croydon, CR0 4YY

Library of Congress Cataloging-in-Publication Data

Names: SanGiovanni, John, author. | Bay-Williams, Jennifer M., author. |
   Serrano, Rosalba, author.
Title: Figuring out fluency - addition and subtraction with whole numbers :
   a classroom companion / John J. SanGiovanni, Jennifer M. Bay-Williams,
   Rosalba Serrano.
Description: Thousand Oaks, California : Corwin Press, Inc., [2022] |
   Includes bibliographical references and index.
Identifiers: LCCN 2021019510 (print) | LCCN 2021019511 (ebook) | ISBN
   9781071825099 (paperback) | ISBN 9781071851593 | ISBN 9781071851586
Subjects: LCSH: Arithmetic--Study and teaching (Elementary) |
   Arithmetic--Study and teaching (Middle school) | Numbers, Natural. |
   Mathematical fluency.
Classification: LCC QA135.6 .S2577 2022 (print) | LCC QA135.6 (ebook) |
   DDC 372.7/2--dc23
LC record available at https://lccn.loc.gov/2021019510
LC ebook record available at https://lccn.loc.gov/2021019511

This book is printed on acid-free paper.

21 22 23 24 25 10 9 8 7 6 5 4 3 2 1

Contents

Visit the companion website at
**resources.corwin.com/FOF/
addsubtractwholenumber**
for downloadable resources.

Preface

Fluency is an equity issue. In written documents and in our daily work, we (mathematics teachers and leaders) communicate that every student must be *fluent* with whole number addition and subtraction, for example. But we haven't even come close to accomplishing this for each and every student. The most recent National Assessment of Educational Progress (NAEP) data, for example, finds that about two-fifths (41%) of the nation's Grade 4 students are at or above proficient and about one-third (34%) of our nation's Grade 8 students at or above proficient (NCES, 2019). We can and must do better! One major reason we haven't been able to develop fluent students is that there are misunderstandings about what fluency really means.

FIGURING OUT FLUENCY

In order to ensure every student develops fluency, we first must:

- Understand what procedural fluency is (and what it isn't),
- Respect fluency, and
- Plan to explicitly teach and assess reasoning strategies.

If you have read our anchor book *Figuring Out Fluency for Mathematics Teaching and Learning*—which we recommend in order to get the most out of *this* classroom companion—you'll remember an in-depth discussion of these topics.

WHAT PROCEDURAL FLUENCY IS AND ISN'T

Like fluency with language, wherein you decide how you want to communicate an idea, fluency in mathematics involves decision-making as you decide how to solve a problem. In our anchor book, we propose the following visual as a way to illustrate the full meaning of fluency.

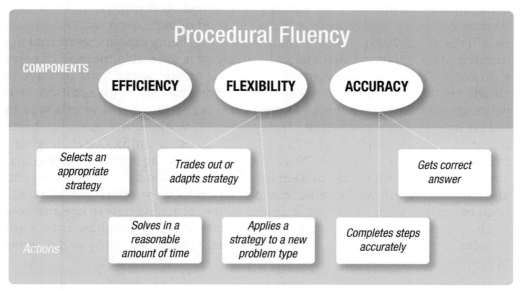

Part 1 of this book explains the elements of this procedural fluency graphic. To cut to the chase, procedural fluency is much more than knowing facts and standard algorithms. Fluency involves higher-level thinking, wherein a person analyzes a problem, considers options for how to solve it, selects an efficient strategy, and accurately enacts that strategy (trading it out for another if it doesn't go well). Decision-making is key and that means you need to have good options to choose from. This book provides instructional and practice activities so that students learn different options (Part 2) and then provides practice activities to help students learn to choose options (Part 3).

RESPECT FLUENCY

We are strong advocates for conceptual understanding. We all must be. But there is not a choice here. Fluency relies on conceptual understanding, and conceptual understanding alone cannot help students fluently navigate computational situations. They go together and must be connected. Instructional activities throughout Part 2 provide opportunities for students to discuss, critique, and justify their thinking, connecting their conceptual understanding to their procedural knowledge and vice versa.

EXPLICITLY TEACH AND ASSESS REASONING STRATEGIES

If every student is to be fluent in whole number addition and subtraction, then every student needs access to the significant strategies for these operations. And there must be opportunities for students to learn how to select the best strategy for a particular problem. For example, students may learn that the Make Hundreds strategy works well when one or both of the addends is close to a hundred (e.g., 495 + 637) but not as well when neither addend is close to a hundred (e.g., 458 + 371). To accomplish this, all three fluency components must have equitable attention in instruction and assessment. This is a major shift from traditional teaching and assessing, which privileges accuracy over the other two components and the standard algorithm over reasoning strategies.

Let's unpack the phrase *explicit strategy instruction*. According to the *Merriam-Webster Dictionary*, *explicit* means "fully revealed or expressed without vagueness" ("Explicit," 2021). In mathematics teaching, being *explicit* means making mathematical relationships visible. A strategy is a flexible method to solve a problem. *Explicit strategy instruction*, then, is engaging students in ways to clearly see how and why a strategy works. For example, with addition, students might compare 100 + 15 and 98 + 17 on the number line as a way to reveal how the Compensation strategy works. With subtraction, students might be asked to explain why 75 − 58 = 77 − 60 using Unifix Cubes, tiny ten-frame cards, or a number line. Proving examples leads to a generalization that you can change both values of a subtraction expression by the same amount, and the answer will be the same (compensation!). Once understood, students need to explore *when* a strategy is a good option. Learning how to use and how to choose strategies *empowers* students to be able to decide how they want to solve a problem, developing a positive mathematics identity and a sense of agency.

USING THIS BOOK

This book is a classroom companion to *Figuring Out Fluency for Mathematics Teaching and Learning*. In that anchor book, we lay out what fluency is, identify the fallacies that stand in the way of a true focus on fluency, and elaborate on necessary foundations for fluency. We also propose the following:

- Seven Significant Strategies across the operations, five of which apply to whole number addition and subtraction

- Eight "automaticies" *beyond* automaticity with basic facts, four of which are relevant to whole number addition and subtraction

- Five ways to engage students in meaningful practice

- Four assessment options that can replace (or at least complement) tests and that focus on real fluency

- Many ways to engage families in supporting their child's fluency

In Part 1 of this book, we revisit some of these ideas in order to connect specifically to whole number addition and subtraction. This section is not a substitute for the anchor book, but rather a brief revisiting of central ideas that serve as reminders of what was fully illustrated, explained, and justified in *Figuring Out Fluency in Mathematics Teaching and Learning*. Hopefully, you have had the chance to read and engage with that content with colleagues *first*, and then Part 1 will help you think about those ideas as they apply to whole number addition and subtraction. Finally, Part 1 includes suggestions for how to use the strategy modules.

Part 2 is focused on explicit instruction of each significant strategy for whole number addition and subtraction. Each module includes the following:

- An overview for your reference and to share with students and colleagues

- A strategy brief for families

- A series of instructional activities, with the final one offering a series of questions to promote discourse about the strategy

- A series of practice activities, including worked examples, routines, games, and center activities that engage students in meaningful and ongoing practice to develop proficiency with that strategy

As you are teaching and find your students are ready to learn a particular strategy, pull this book off the shelf, go to the related module, and access the activities and ready-to-use resources. While the modules are sequenced in a developmental order overall, the order and focus on each strategy may vary depending on your grade and your students' experiences. Additionally, teaching within or across modules does not happen all at once; rather, activities can be woven into your instruction regularly, over time.

Part 3 is about becoming truly fluent—developing flexibility and efficiency with addition and subtraction of whole numbers. Filled with more routines, games, and centers, the focus here is on students *choosing* to use the strategies that make sense to them in a given situation. Part 3 also provides assessment tools to monitor students' fluency. As you are teaching and find your students are needing opportunities to choose from among the strategies they are learning, pull this book off the shelf and select an activity from Part 3.

In the Appendix, you will find lists of all the activities in order to help you easily locate what you are looking for by strategy or by type of resource.

This book can be used to complement or supplement any published mathematics program or district-created program. As we noted earlier, elementary mathematics has tended to fall short in its attention to efficiency and flexibility (and the related Fluency Actions illustrated in the earlier graphic). This book provides a large collection of activities to address these neglected components of fluency. Note that this book is part of a series that explores other operations and other numbers. You may also be interested in *Figuring Out Fluency for Whole Number Multiplication and Division* as well as the classroom companion books for decimal and fraction operations.

WHO IS THIS BOOK FOR?

With nearly 100 activities and a companion website with resources ready to download, this book is designed to support classroom teachers as they advance their students' fluency with whole number addition and subtraction. Special education teachers will find the explicit strategy instruction, as well as the additional practice, useful in supporting their students. Mathematics coaches and specialists can use this book for professional learning and to provide instructional resources to the classroom teachers they support. Mathematics supervisors and curriculum leads can use this book to help them assess fluency aspects of their mathematics curriculum and fill potential gaps in resources and understanding. Teacher preparation programs can use this book to galvanize preservice teachers' understanding of fluency and provide teacher candidates with a wealth of classroom-ready resources to use during internships and as they begin their career.

Acknowledgments

Just as there are many components to fluency, there are certainly many components to having a book like this come to fruition. The first component is the researchers and advocates who have defined procedural fluency and effective practices that support it. Research on student learning is hard work, as is defining effective teaching practices, and so we want to begin by acknowledging this work. We have learned from these scholars, and we ground our ideas in their findings. It is on their shoulders that we stand. Second are the teachers and their students who have taken up "real" fluency practices and shared their experiences with us. We would not have taken on this book had we not seen firsthand how a focus on procedural fluency in classrooms truly transforms students' learning and shapes their mathematics identities. It is truly inspiring! Additionally, the testimonies from many teachers about their own learning experiences as students and as teachers helped crystalize for us the facts and fallacies in this book. A third component to bringing this book to fruition was the family support to allow us to actually do the work. We are all grateful to our family members—expressed in our personal statements that follow—who supported us 24/7 as we wrote during a pandemic.

From Jennifer: I am forever grateful to my husband, Mitch, who is supportive and helpful in every way. I also thank my children, MacKenna and Nicolas, who often offer reactions and also endure a lot of talk about mathematics, including hearing every person at a family reunion talk about how they would solve $48 + 49$. And that leads to my gratitude to my extended family—a mother who served on the school board for 13 years and helped me make it to a second year of teaching and a father who was a statistician and leader and helped me realize I could do "uncomfortable" things. My siblings—an accountant, a high school math teacher, and a university statistician—and their children have all supported my work on this book and the others in this series.

From John: I want to thank my family—especially my wife—who, as always, endure and support the ups and downs of taking on a new project. Thank you to Jenny and Rosalba for being exceptional partners. And thank you for dealing with my random thoughts, tangent conversations, and fantastic humor. As always, a heartfelt thank you to certain math friends and mentors for opportunities, faith in me, and support over the years. And thank you to my own math teachers who let me do math "my way," even if it wasn't "the way" back then.

From Rosalba: I want to thank my three boys, Daniel, Dylan, and Declan. All of the long days and hard work I do is to make the world a better place for you. Thank you for being so patient with your Madre and listening to countless math conversations. To John and Jenny, I cannot express enough thanks. Thank you for your advice, support, and encouragement throughout this process. I am forever grateful for this learning experience and the opportunity you have given me.

A fourth component is vision and writing support. We are so grateful to Corwin for recognizing the importance of defining and implementing procedural fluency in the mathematics classroom. Our editor and publisher, Erin Null, has gone above and beyond as a partner in the work, ensuring that our ideas are as well stated and useful as possible. The entire editing team at Corwin has been creative, thorough, helpful, and supportive.

As with fluency, no component is more important than another, and without any component, there is no book, so to the researchers, teachers, family, and editing team, thank you. We are so grateful.

PUBLISHER'S ACKNOWLEDGMENTS

Corwin gratefully acknowledges the contributions of the following reviewers:

Becky Evans
Grades 3–5 Math Teacher Leader
Lincoln Public Schools

Jamie Fraser
Math Consultant
Developer and Educational Distributer
Bound2Learn

Sarah Gat
Instructional Coach
Upper Grand District School Board

Kristine M. Gettelman
Instructional Designer
CenterPoint Education

Christina Hawley
Grade 1 and Grade 2 Teacher

Cathy Martin
Associate Chief of Academics
Denver Public Schools

Carly Morales
Instructional Coach
District 93

Margie Pearse
Math Coach

Nicole Rigelman
Professor of Mathematics Education
Portland State University

Meghan Schofield
Third-Grade Teacher

About the Authors

John J. SanGiovanni is a mathematics supervisor in Howard County, Maryland. There, he leads mathematics curriculum development, digital learning, assessment, and professional development. John is an adjunct professor and coordinator of the Elementary Mathematics Instructional Leadership graduate program at McDaniel College. He is an author and national mathematics curriculum and professional learning consultant. John is a frequent speaker at national conferences and institutes. He is active in state and national professional organizations, recently serving on the board of directors for the National Council of Teachers of Mathematics (NCTM) and currently as the president of the Maryland Council of Supervisors of Mathematics.

Jennifer M. Bay-Williams is a professor of mathematics education at the University of Louisville, where she teaches preservice teachers, emerging elementary mathematics specialists, and doctoral students in mathematics education. She has authored numerous books as well as many journal articles, many of which focus on procedural fluency (and other aspects of effective mathematics teaching and learning). Jennifer is a frequent presenter at national and state conferences and works with schools and districts around the world. Her national leadership includes having served as a member of the NCTM Board of Directors, on the TODOS: Mathematics for All Board of Directors, and as president and secretary of the Association of Mathematics Teacher Educators (AMTE).

Rosalba Serrano is an elementary mathematics consultant in New York and is the founder of Zenned Math, where she provides online professional development and coaching for elementary mathematics teachers. Rosalba has used her experience as a classroom teacher and mathematics coach to support teachers in deepening their understanding of mathematics and their use of effective teaching practices. A frequent speaker at both regional and national conferences, Rosalba is also active in mathematics organizations such as the NCTM, where she contributes to multiple committees. She has also worked as a professional development facilitator for various mathematics organizations and consults as a math editor for a number of publishing companies.

PART 1

FIGURING OUT FLUENCY

Key Ideas

WHAT IS FLUENCY WITH WHOLE NUMBER ADDITION AND SUBTRACTION?

To set the stage for figuring out fluency for whole number addition and subtraction, take a moment to do some math. Find the solution to each of these.

58 + 35	584 − 262	479 + 241
363 − 180	1,499 + 707	1,400 − 1,268

How did you find the sums and differences? Did you use the same approach or strategy for each? Did you move between different strategies? Did you change out a strategy based on the numbers within the problem? Did you start with one strategy and shift to another? You likely said "yes" to all of these questions because you fluently add and subtract whole numbers. Yet another reader can answer "yes" to each of these questions as well but solve each problem differently. This is true because fluency is a way of thinking rather than a way of doing. Thinking is unique to each individual. Thinking is grounded in parameters but its execution is left to the understanding, preference, and creativity of each thinker.

Of course, there are strategies used most frequently for certain problems (based on the numbers in the problem), but even in those examples, efficient alternatives are likely. For example, 1,499 + 707 may seem like a problem that "fits" Compensation: change 1,499 to 1,500 (add 1), add 1,500 + 707 (2,207), and adjust (subtract 1) to get 2,206 (Module 4). But a Partial Sums approach may "jump out" to another person who sees the problem this way: 1,400 + 700 (2,100) and 99 + 7 (106), combined is 2,206 (Module 3). Which method is closer to your way of thinking? Or did you think about it differently?

TEACHING TAKEAWAY

Real fluency is the ability to select efficient strategies; to adapt, modify, or change out strategies; and to find solutions with accuracy.

Real fluency is the ability to select efficient strategies; to adapt, modify, or change out strategies; and to find solutions with accuracy. Real fluency is not the act of replicating someone else's steps or procedures for doing mathematics. It is the act of thinking, reasoning, and doing mathematics on one's own. Before fluency can be taught well, you must understand what fluency is and why it matters.

Procedural fluency is an umbrella term that includes basic fact fluency and computational fluency (see Figure 1). *Basic fact fluency* attends to fluently adding,

FIGURE 1 ● The Relationship of Different Fluency Terms in Mathematics

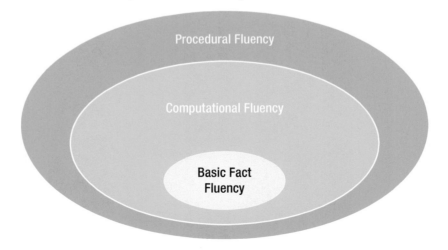

subtracting, multiplying, and dividing single-digit numbers. *Computational fluency* refers to the fluency in four operations across number types (whole numbers, fractions, etc.), regardless of the magnitude of the number. Procedural fluency encompasses both basic fact fluency and computational fluency, plus other procedures like finding equivalent fractions.

Beyond being an umbrella term that encompasses basic fact and computational fluency, procedural fluency is well defined as solving procedures efficiently, flexibly, and accurately (Kilpatrick, Swafford, & Findell, 2001; National Council of Teachers of Mathematics, 2014). These three **components** are defined as follows:

Efficiency: solving a procedure in a reasonable amount of time by selecting an appropriate strategy and readily implementing that strategy

Flexibility: knowing multiple procedures and can apply or adapt strategies to solve procedural problems (Baroody & Dowker, 2003; Star, 2005)

Accuracy: correctly solving a procedure

Strategies are not the same as algorithms. Strategies are general methods that are flexible in design, compared to algorithms that are established steps implemented the same way across problems.

To focus on fluency, we need specific observable actions that we can look for in what students are doing in order to ensure they are developing fluency. We have identified six such actions. The three components and six Fluency Actions, and their relationships, are illustrated in Figure 2.

FIGURE 2 • Procedural Fluency Components, Actions, and Checks for Reasonableness

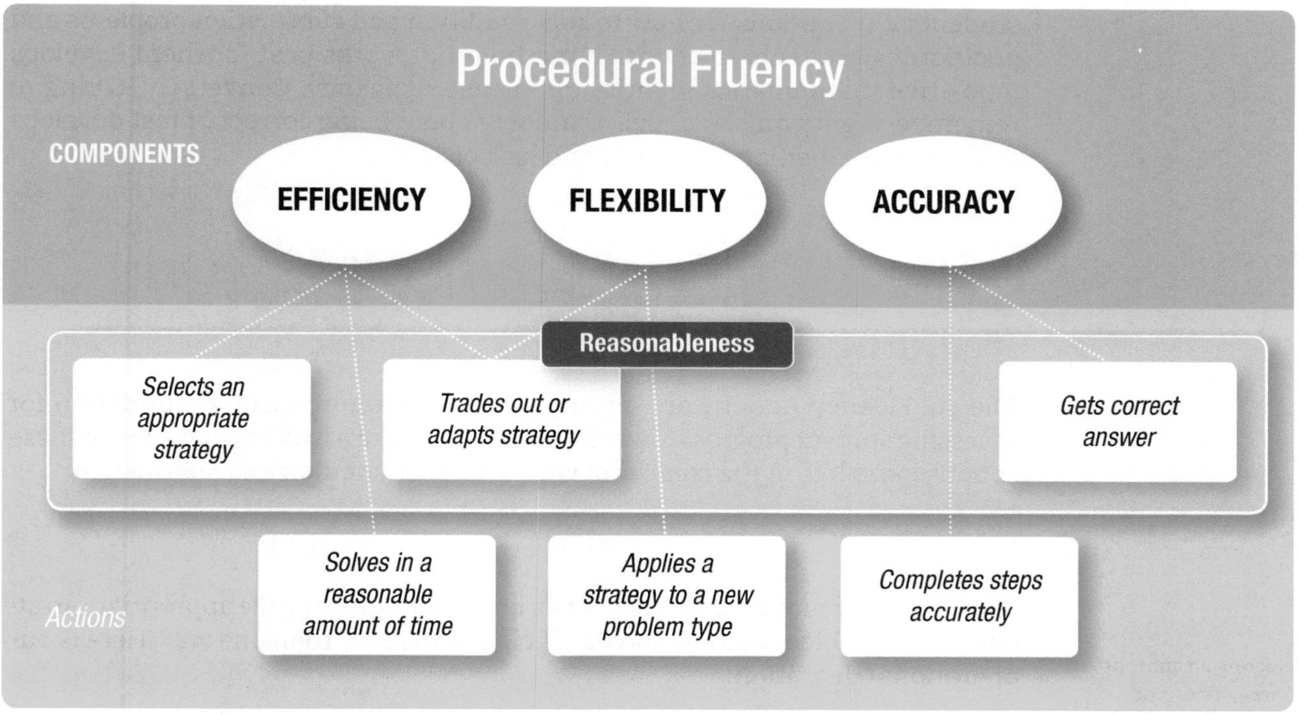

Source: Adapted with permission from D. Spangler & J. Wanko (Eds.), *Enhancing Classroom Practice with Research behind Principles to Actions*, copyright 2017, by the National Council of Teachers of Mathematics. All rights reserved.

Three of the six Fluency Actions (should) attend to reasonableness. Fluency Actions and reasonableness are described later in Part 1, but first, it is important to consider why this "bigger" (comprehensive) view of fluency matters.

WHY FOCUS ON FLUENCY FOR WHOLE NUMBER ADDITION AND SUBTRACTION?

There are two key reasons why it's important to focus on fluency with whole number addition and subtraction. First, it is a critical foundation for ensuring that students fully realize procedural fluency in general, with all kinds of numbers. Fluency with whole numbers begins with developing fluency with single-digit addition and subtraction (the basic facts) and seeing how strategies such as Making 10 can be transferred to making a 30 or a 200 in order to add whole numbers efficiently (we call this generalized strategy Make Tens; basic facts are addressed in more detail later in Part 1). Fluency with addition and subtraction is a *necessity* for developing fluency with multiplication and division. For example, an efficient way to solve 9×35 is to think 10×35 (350) and subtract a group of 35 (315). This final step (350 – 35) requires subtraction fluency. A student needs to have a quick—often mental—way to do this subtraction, perhaps Counting Back, subtracting 30, and then subtracting 5. Fluency with whole number addition and subtraction is also a necessary foundation for fluency with rational numbers. Students will adapt their reasoning strategies with whole numbers to become fluent in adding and subtracting fractions and decimals (e.g., adapting Make Tens to Make a Whole). These connections are a focus of our anchor book, *Figuring Out Fluency in Mathematics Teaching and Learning* (hereafter titled *Figuring Out Fluency*).

Second and most importantly, developing fluency is an equity issue. Equipping students with options for how to solve addition and subtraction problems and positioning students to choose a method that works best for them develops a positive mathematics identity and sense of agency. Conversely, trying to remember algorithms and feeling anxiety about being correct or fast develops a negative mathematics identity and lack of agency.

WHAT DO FLUENCY ACTIONS LOOK LIKE FOR WHOLE NUMBER ADDITION AND SUBTRACTION?

The six Fluency Actions are observable and therefore form a foundation for assessing student progress toward fluency. Let's take a look at what each of these actions looks like in the context of whole number addition and subtraction.

FLUENCY ACTION 1: Select an Appropriate Strategy

Selecting *an* appropriate strategy does not mean selecting *the* appropriate strategy. Many problems can be solved efficiently in more than one way. Here is our operational definition: Of the available strategies, the one the student opts to use gets to a solution in about as many steps and/or about as much time as other appropriate options.

Consider 479 + 241. One could Count On from 479 (Figure 3a), Use Partial Sums (Figure 3b), or Make Hundreds (Figure 3c). Each of these strategies is appropriate for this problem but may not be as appropriate for other problems such as 500 + 363 or 299 + 476. Notice that this Fluency Action is one of three connected to *reasonableness*. Within this action is noticing when a strategy "fits" the numbers in the problem.

FIGURE 3 ● Adding 479 + 241

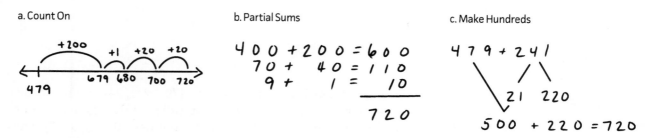

a. Count On

b. Partial Sums

c. Make Hundreds

A strategy cannot be used until it is understood. Once understood, a strategy becomes part of a student's repertoire of options and they are then able to select the strategy.

Importantly, we name strategies so that we can talk about them. But one approach may fit within various types of strategies and have different names. For example, solving 65 + 59 as 50 + 50 + 5 + 9 may be using Make Hundreds thinking, Compensation thinking, or Partial Sums thinking. The focus must be on the ideas (not the naming of the strategy).

FLUENCY ACTION 2: Solve in a Reasonable Amount of Time

There is no set amount of time that should be expected for solving any whole number addition or subtraction problem. Students should be able to work through a problem without getting stuck or lost. The amount of time is relative to the student's grade and mathematical maturity. Keep in mind that appropriate strategies can be carried out in inefficient, unreasonable ways. For example, Figure 3a shows counting on in chunks. But a student might count on by doing 24 jumps of tens and ones, which is not a method to solve 479 + 241 in a reasonable amount of time.

FLUENCY ACTION 3: Trade Out or Adapt a Strategy

As strategies are better understood, students are able to adapt them or swap them out for another more efficient strategy. Students first learning to use the Count On strategy may think of 241 as 24 jumps of 10. They should soon begin to *adapt* that strategy by counting in larger chunks as shown in Figure 4.

FIGURE 4 ● Counting by Hundreds, Tens, and Ones

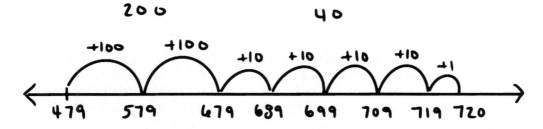

Rather than adapt the Count On strategy, a student might *trade out* the strategy for a Make Hundreds strategy, reasoning that they can move 21 over to rethink the sum as 500 + 220 (see Figure 3c). Notice that this Fluency Action is one of three connected to *reasonableness*. Within this action is noticing how the use of the strategy is going. If it isn't going well or if a student is getting bogged down, then the strategy needs to be adapted or traded for another, more efficient option.

FLUENCY ACTION 4: Apply a Strategy to a New Problem Type

The Use Hundreds work shows how, when adding 479 + 241, 241 can be decomposed in a clever way to make 500 from 479. That individual's first experience with Make a 10 was likely to work with basic facts that use 10 (e.g., 9 + 7). They then learned to use the Make Tens strategy when adding 69 + 17 (69 + 1 + 16) and eventually to use the Make Hundreds strategy to make 500 when adding 490 + 27 (490 + 10 + 17). Their foundational understanding of Make a 10 was expanded and applied to new problem types. In time, this strategy will be applied to using a whole when adding fractions or decimals.

FLUENCY ACTIONS 5 AND 6: Complete Steps Accurately and Get Correct Answers

These two Fluency Actions are about accuracy. An error at the end of a problem may be due to an error in how a strategy was enacted. For example, in using Compensation for 64 – 29, a student changes the problem to 64 – 30 to get 34 and then *subtracts* 1 from the answer (resulting in the incorrect answer of 33) rather than *adds* 1 (resulting in the correct answer of 35). This incorrect answer is due to a misconception of the steps in implementing the Compensation strategy. Conversely, a student may enact a strategy accurately but make a computational error. The student's work in Figure 5 is a good example of this.

FIGURE 5 ● Counting On Incorrectly

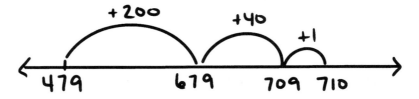

Fluency Action 6 is one of three connected to *reasonableness*. Within this action is noticing if your answer makes sense. While reasonableness has been woven into the discussion of Fluency Actions, it is critical to fluency and warrants more discussion.

REASONABLENESS

As described earlier, reasonableness is more than "checking your answer." Reasonableness occurs in three of the six Fluency Actions as shown in Figure 2 and described within the related Fluency Actions. Let's revisit the sum 479 + 241. Counting on to solve 479 + 241 is a reasonable strategy choice (Action 1). Carrying it out reasonably means to add on chunks of 241 (a student should notice that if they are counting by tens, the strategy is not going well and adapt their approach) (Action 3). Finally, 720 is a reasonable answer (Action 6). Checking to see if an answer is reasonable can be determined in (at least) three different ways:

1. You might estimate the sum to be about 700 by rounding each addend.

2. You might estimate it to be about 740 using friendly numbers (500 and 240).

3. You might think about it being in the range of 600 (400 + 200) and 800 (500 + 300).

It takes time to develop reasonableness. It should be practiced and discussed as often as possible. Students can develop reasonableness by practicing three moves (a match to the Fluency Actions 1, 3, and 6).

THREE 'Cs' OF REASONABLENESS

Choose: Choose a strategy that is efficient based on the numbers in the problem.
Change: Change the strategy if it is proving to be overly complex or unsuccessful.
Check: Check to make sure the result makes sense.

You can encourage and support student thinking about reasonableness by providing Choose, Change, Check reflection cards (see Figure 6). These cards can be adapted into anchor charts for students to use while working on problems or during class discussions about adding and subtracting.

FIGURE 6 ● Choose, Change, Check Reflection Card for Students

CHECKS FOR REASONABLENESS		
Choose	Change	Check
Is this something I can do in my head? What strategy makes sense for these numbers?	Is my strategy going well or should I try a different approach? Does my answer so far seem reasonable?	Is my answer close to what I anticipated it might be? How might I check my answer?

Icon sources: Choose by iStock.com/Enis Aksoy; Change by iStock.com/Sigit Mulyo Utomo; Check by iStock.com/Indigo Diamond.

online resources ⇗ This resource can be downloaded at **resources.corwin.com/FOF/addsubtractwholenumber**.

WHAT FOUNDATIONS DO STUDENTS NEED TO DEVELOP FLUENCY WITH ADDITION AND SUBTRACTION?

To develop fluency, students need a strong foundation in five domains:

- *Conceptual understanding*: knowing the meaning of the operations
- *Properties*: being able to use the operations in order to manipulate numbers and retain equivalence
- *Utilities*: small skills that make a big difference, such as knowing how far 9 is from 10
- *Computational estimation*: being able to quickly and flexibly determine a "close" answer
- *Basic facts*: single-digit addition and subtraction facts that are needed for multidigit work

Rushing students to strategy instruction before these foundations are firmly in place can be disastrous.

CONCEPTUAL UNDERSTANDING

Developing fluency from conceptual understanding begins with including concrete experiences for students so they can make sense of the quantities. Hence, developing fluency *begins* with stories. It is a mistake to save story problems as an application, as stories give students a context from which they can reason.

Story problems must vary in two ways:

1. Type of situation (a join story, a part–part–whole story)
2. What is unknown in the story (the initial quantity, the change, or the result)

If you audit a page of "word problems" for addition and subtraction, you will likely find that "join" stories for addition and "separate" stories for subtraction are over-represented, and part–part–whole and compare stories are under-represented. Audit again for what is unknown in the story and you will likely find that most or all of the stories read as "result unknown." When stories fall into the same style, students overgeneralize how to interpret the stories. Figure 7 can be used as a resource to be sure you are varying your story types (for example, you can tally which types of stories you are telling as part of action research).

FIGURE 7 ● Addition and Subtraction Situations

ADDITION AND SUBTRACTION SITUATIONS			
Join	**Separate**	**Compare**	**Part–part–whole**
Story is about something being added to an original amount.	Story is about something being removed from the original amount.	Story compares two quantities.	Story is about combining different types of objects.
Ex: AJ had ____ books. She got ____ books. She has a total of ____ books.	Ex: AJ had ____ books. She gave away ____ books. Now she has a total of ____ books.	Ex: AJ has ____ books. Ian has ____ books. AJ has ____ more/less than Ian.	Ex: AJ has ____ fiction books and ____ nonfiction books. The total of her books is ____.

Beyond considering story type and missing values, here are few important ideas to keep in mind:

1. Stories need to be *relevant* to students, meaning that students are familiar with the context and it is interesting to students.

2. Avoid key-word strategies for solving story problems so that students must make sense of the problem and how addition or subtraction can be used to find a solution.

3. Use representations that are true to the situation (e.g., if comparing heights, use a vertical number line) until students have a deep understanding and are able to work symbolically and move between representations and tell explicitly how they are related.

In addition to stories, visuals provide concrete, conceptual beginnings for students. For example, young children count collections of objects in order to start learning to skip-count (Franke, Kazemi, & Turrou, 2018). Counting objects progresses to counting visuals and representations such as a Hundred Chart or number line, which eventually leads to abstract counting strategies such as the Count On/Count Back strategy. Hundred Charts and number lines similarly support the other reasoning strategies, such as Make Tens (or Hundreds) and Compensation.

PROPERTIES AND UTILITIES FOR STRATEGIC COMPETENCE

In addition to conceptual foundations, fluency is grounded in using properties of the operations and a few other skills that we refer to as "utilities" because students must utilize them in their reasoning. First, fluency with addition relies heavily on students using the commutative and associative properties of addition. Note that knowing properties does not equal using properties. It is *not* useful to have students simply name the associative property. It is absolutely necessary that students *utilize* this property in solving problems efficiently.

TEACHING TAKEAWAY
Knowing properties does not equal using properties.

For example, in the following problems, students look to rearrange these numbers (mentally or in writing) as they look for pairs that add to benchmark numbers:

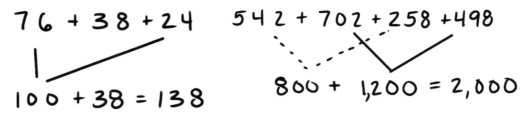

The first problem is the commutative property in use:

$$76 + 38 + 24 = 76 + 24 + 38$$

The second problem uses both the commutative and associative properties:

$$542 + 702 + 258 + 498 = 542 + 258 + 702 + 498$$

$$= (542 + 258) + (702 + 498)$$

$$= 800 + 1,200$$

See Chapter 3 (pp. 47–75) of *Figuring Out Fluency* for more about foundations and good beginnings for fluency.

Beyond the properties is a short list of utilities that support fluency, which is presented in Figure 8.

FIGURE 8 ● Utilities for Strategic Competence With Addition and Subtraction

UTILITY	WHAT IT IS	RELATIONSHIP TO FLUENCY
Distance From a 10	Knowing that 9 is 1 away from 10 (and 8 is 2 away and so on).	Knowing how far a number (e.g., 5, 6, 7, 8, 9) is from 10 is necessary to implement reasoning strategies, in particular Counting On/Back/Up, Make Tens, and Use Compensation.
Composing and Decomposing Numbers Flexibly	Understanding diverse, flexible ways to compose and decompose, including but not limited to place value decomposition.	Flexibly decomposing numbers supports strategy selection and facility with any of the strategies.
Part–Part–Whole	Understanding that addition and subtraction are based on parts making up a whole.	While the label has two parts and one whole, the reality is that it could be three parts or more. In other words, a part can be broken into parts in order to make a 10 or 100, or other benchmark number that will make adding or subtracting easier.
Skip-Counting	Skip-counting by tens, hundreds, and thousands, including multiples of these.	Efficiency comes from skip-counting in chunks rather than singles. This applies to different strategies, including Counting On/Back/Up and Partial Sums.

COMPUTATIONAL ESTIMATION

Just like computation, there are strategies for estimation and the use of those strategies should be *flexible*. For addition and subtraction of whole numbers, students might use any of these methods:

1. *Rounding*: Flexible rounding means that one or both numbers might be rounded. Students may round to the nearest number or they may round one number up and one number down to have a more accurate estimate.

Rounding is a well-known strategy but is often approached in a step-by-step manner, which can interfere with the point of estimating—getting a quick idea of what the answer will be close to. Use conceptual language, such as, "Which tens/hundreds/thousands is that number close to?" Help students understand that they choose how to round. For example, rounding both 2,403 + 3,495 down to the nearest thousand will give a very low estimate, whereas rounding one up and one down gives a closer estimate.

2. *Front-end estimation*: In its most basic form, students just add or subtract the largest place value. More flexibly, though, students may use the largest two place values, or adjust their estimate because of what they notice with the rest of the numbers. Front-end estimation is *quick*. For example, 74 – 36 is 40 and 387 + 635 is 900. To adjust, take a quick look to the right and decide to keep the estimate or adjust. For 387 + 635, there's at least 100 more, so go up to 1,000.

3. *Compatible numbers*: With flexibility in mind, students change one or both of the numbers to a nearby number so that the numbers are easy to add or subtract. For example, estimating the sum of 283 and 725 could be 300 and 700 to make 1,000, or it could be 275 and 725, which is also 1,000. Compatibles are particularly useful with subtraction. Consider estimating 3,456 – 1,890. Compatible alternatives might be 3,400 – 1,400, 3,500 – 1,500, or 3,500 – 2,000.

DEVELOPING BASIC FACT FLUENCY

The teaching of basic facts must attend to conceptual understanding and strategies for reasoning rather than rote instruction (Bay-Williams & Kling, 2019; O'Connell & SanGiovanni, 2015). Reasons to focus on *strategies* when teaching the basic facts (as opposed to memorizing) include the following:

1. It is well established across many studies that students actually learn and retain their facts better when they focus on conceptual understanding versus memorization. In fact, students don't just learn and retain their facts better, they perform better in math *in general* (e.g., Baroody, Purpura, Eiland, Reid, & Paliwal, 2016; Brendefur, Strother, Thiede, & Appleton, 2015; Jordan, Kaplan, Ramineni & Locuniak, 2009; Locuniak & Jordan, 2008; Purpura, Baroody, Eiland, & Reid, 2016).

2. Students need to know and use these strategies to support whole number addition and subtraction (as well as decimal and fraction operations!). In our *Figuring Out Fluency* anchor book, we elaborate more on the key strategies and ideas for effectively developing basic fact fluency.

3. Students who learn to use and choose strategies for basic facts develop confidence. Students who memorize often develop anxiety. A student who knows how to generate an answer to a sum such as 8 + 7 (beyond counting) doesn't have to worry if they forget the fact. This sense of agency is critical to student success in mathematics!

Figure 9 lists the basic fact strategies for addition and subtraction. To be clear, automaticity is the goal for learning basic facts. Students become automatic through learning the strategies and practicing them over and over again. In so doing, students develop automaticity with the facts and with implementing the strategies. Examples are illustrated in Figure 10. Keep in mind that there are many ways to implement a reasoning strategy, and only one way is shown for each example.

FIGURE 9 ● Reasoning Strategies for Basic Fact Addition and Subtraction

STRATEGY NAME	HOW THE STRATEGY WORKS	EXAMPLE STUDENT TALK
Addition	**Example: 8 + 6**	
Near Doubles	Student looks for a double they know that is similar to the problem. In this case, 8 + 8, 6 + 6, or even 7 + 7.	That's 14: 6 plus 6 plus 2.
Making 10	Student moves some from one addend to the other so that one addend is 10.	It's 14. I moved 2 over and thought 10 + 4.
Pretend-a-10 (Compensation)	Student pretends the larger addend is 10, adds, then adjusts the answer.	It's 14. Well, 10 and 6 is 16, and I have to take two away, so that's 14.
Subtraction	**Example: 14 − 9**	
Think Addition	Student thinks how to get from the subtrahend (9) to the minuend (14) [9 + ___ = 14]. *Note: Subtraction as compare*	It's 5. I pictured a number line and jumped up 1 to 10 and then 4 more.
Down Under 10	Student jumps from the minuend (14) to 10 and then jumps the rest of the subtrahend (9). *Note: Subtraction as take away*	It's 5. I broke 9 into 4 and 5. I jumped down 4 to 10, and then 5 more to 5.
Take From 10	Student subtracts the subtrahend (9) from 10, then adds on the extra ones from the minuend. *Note: Subtraction as take away*	I got 5. I thought of 14 as 10 and 4, subtracted 9 from 10 and got 1, and added the 4 back on and it's 5.

Except for Near Doubles, each of these strategies evolves directly to the strategies that are the focus of Part 2 of this book when students deal with whole numbers. You can see this transformation in the examples in Figure 10.

FIGURE 10 ● How Basic Fact Strategies Grow Into General Reasoning Strategies

REASONING STRATEGY	EXAMPLES WITH MULTIDIGIT NUMBERS
Making 10 becomes **Make Tens** (Hundreds, etc.)	39 + 28 = 40 + 27 97 + 35 = 100 + 32 395 + 784 = 400 + 779
Pretend-a-10 becomes **Compensation**	39 + 28 → 40 + 30 − 3 → 70 − 3 → 67 3,499 + 5,148 → 3,500 + 5,148 − 1 → 8,648 − 1 → 8,647
Think Addition becomes **Counting Up (or Back)**, in general, finding the difference between the two numbers	89 − 75 → 75 to 85 (10) to 89 (4) → jumps add to 14 615 − 582 → 582 to 600 (18) to 615 (15) → jumps add to 33
Down Under 10 becomes **Counting Back**, in general using skip-counting to take away an amount	52 − 8 → 52 − 2 (to 50) − 6 → 44 52 − 28 → 52 − 2 (to 50) − 20 (to 30) − 6 (to 24) 3,450 − 1,650 → 3,450 − 450 (to 3000) − 1,200 (to 1,800)
Take From 10 becomes **Partial Differences**, with the subtrahend taken from the largest place value. This becomes flexible and blends in **Compensation**, too.	52 − 28 → 50 − 28 (22) → 2 + 22 (24) 456 − 280 → 400 − 280 → 120 + 56 → 176

WHAT AUTOMATICITIES DO STUDENTS NEED BEYOND THEIR BASIC FACTS?

Unlike the foundation of conceptual understanding, automaticities are not pre-requisites for, but coincide with strategy instruction. For example, automaticity with basic facts (just discussed) begins with strategy instruction and leads to eventual automaticity with the facts. But there are automaticities beyond the basic facts that support student reasoning!

Automaticity is the ability to complete a task with little or no attention to process. Little thought, if any, is given to skills that are automatic (Cheind & Schneider, 2012). We consider automaticities to be those skills that a fluent person can do without much attention to process. For example, you know that if you need to break 2 off of a 6, there is 4 left. Subtraction or a number line is not needed; it is intuitive or reflexive. Figure 11 identifies automaticities that complements strategies for adding and subtracting whole numbers. Of course, this is not a complete list. These automaticities are strengthened through strategy instruction (and conversely, having these automaticities strengthens students' capacities to use strategies).

See Chapter 5 (pp. 107–129) of *Figuring Out Fluency* for more about automaticities for fluency.

FIGURE 11 ● Automaticities for Adding and Subtracting Whole Numbers

AUTOMATICITY	WHAT IT IS	HOW IT COMPLEMENTS STRATEGY INSTRUCTION?
Basic facts	Quickly recognizing how a problem relates to a basic fact (e.g., 3 + 8 relates to 30 + 80).	Identifying relationships to basic facts helps students consider which numbers to decompose and how to decompose them.
Breaking apart all numbers through 10	Being able to quickly decompose any number through 10, which includes breaking the number into more than two parts.	Decomposing numbers flexibly and with automaticity helps students select and carry out a strategy.
Base-10 combinations	Being able to quickly find combinations of 10 and multiples of 10, including hundreds.	Recognizing combinations of tens and multiples enables students to accurately carry out strategies (especially Make Tens/Hundreds, Use Partials, and Compensation).

WHAT ARE THE SIGNIFICANT STRATEGIES FOR ADDING AND SUBTRACTING WHOLE NUMBERS?

Teaching strategies beyond the common algorithms has been a challenge, as there has been pushback and criticism from families and in social media. Two questions require attention:

1. Why do students need strategies when they can use the standard algorithm?

One way to quickly respond to this question is to share an example for which the standard algorithm takes much more time than an alternative. For example, 98 + 99 or 301 – 295. Why learn other methods? Because many problems can be solved more efficiently another way. Fluent students look for efficient methods; if students are limited in the methods they are taught, they have little to choose from, which limits flexibility and efficiency.

2. What strategies are worthy of attention?

TEACHING TAKEAWAY
Students don't need to constantly learn dozens of new strategies, but rather connect how the key strategies they learned for basic facts are transferred to other numbers.

Let's just take some pressure off here. The list is short, and we must help students see that they are not necessarily learning a *new* strategy, but they are applying a strategy they learned with basic facts and transferring it to other numbers. In *Figuring Out Fluency* we propose Seven Significant Strategies. Of these, five relate to adding and/or subtracting whole numbers and they are listed in Figure 12.

FIGURE 12 ● Reasoning Strategies for Adding and Subtracting Whole Numbers

REASONING STRATEGIES	RELEVANT OPERATIONS
1. Count On/Count Back (Module 1)	Addition and Subtraction
2. Make Tens (Module 2)	Addition
3. Partial Sums and Differences (Module 3)	Addition and Subtraction
4. Compensation (Module 4)	Addition and Subtraction
5. Think Addition (Module 5)	Subtraction

To be clear, using connecting cubes or a number line is *not* a strategy. It is a representation. If a student subtracts using connecting cubes or a number line, they are implementing a strategy—perhaps Count Back or Think Addition. When a student says, "I used a number line," ask *how* they used it—then you will learn what strategy they used. Teaching for fluency means that each of these strategies is explicitly taught to students. We teach students to *use* the strategy, and then we give students many opportunities to engage in *choosing* strategies (Part 3 of this book). Explicitly teaching a strategy does not mean turning the strategy into an algorithm. Strategies require flexible thinking. Each module provides instructional ideas and practice to ensure students become adept at using each strategy flexibly. There is also a module on **standard algorithms** (Module 6), so that they are integrated into the use of strategies.

HOW DO I USE THE PART 2 MODULES TO TEACH, PRACTICE, AND ASSESS STRATEGIES?

Part 2 is a set of modules, each one focused on understanding why a specific reasoning strategy works and learning how to use it well. The six modules in Part 2 each have a consistent format. First, each module provides an overview of the strategy—unpacking what it is, how it works, and when it is useful. Then, each module provides a series of teaching activities for explicit strategy instruction, followed by a collection of practice activities, including routines, games, and centers.

EXPLICIT STRATEGY INSTRUCTION

Strategies must be explicitly taught so that students understand them and can use them. Each module provides teaching activities for explicit instruction. The activities are designed so that you can modify and extend them as needed. Any one activity might form the focus of your instruction over the course of multiple lessons. Keep in mind that you can swap out tools and representations as well as adjust the numbers within the task.

The last teaching activity in each module is a collection of *investigation prompts* that you can use to develop reasoning and understanding of the strategy. Each investigation prompt itself can easily become a core instructional task.

We intend for students to work with instructional activities in collaborative partner or group settings. We encourage you to let students make their own meaning and to make mistakes. After students engage in the activities, a group discussion is needed to focus student thinking on the concepts within the strategy, how the strategy works, and the different ways a strategy might be carried out.

QUALITY PRACTICE

Students need access to quality practice that is not a worksheet. Quality practice is focused on a strategy, varied in type of engagement, processed by the student to make sense of what they did, and connected to what they are learning.

Each practice section begins with **worked examples.** Worked examples are opportunities for students to attend to the thinking involved with a strategy, without solving the problem themselves. We feature three types to get at all components of fluency:

See Chapter 6 (pp. 130– 153) of *Figuring Out Fluency* for more about quality practice.

1. *Correctly worked example*: efficiency (selects an appropriate strategy) and flexibility (applies strategy to a new problem type)

2. *Partially worked example*: efficiency (selects an appropriate strategy) and accuracy (completes steps accurately; gets correct answer)

3. *Incorrectly worked example*: accuracy (completes steps accurately; gets correct answer)

Also, comparing two correctly worked examples is very effective in helping students learn to choose efficient methods. Throughout the modules are dozens of examples, which can be used as worked examples (and adapted to other similar worked examples). Your worked examples can be from a fictional "student" or authentic student work. Some of the prompts from teaching the strategy section are, in fact, worked examples.

The remaining practice activities include routines, games, and centers. Each activity provides a brief "About the Activity" statement to help you quickly match what your students need with a meaningful activity. General resources, including number cards, mini ten-frame cards, addition charts, and more, are also available for download on the companion website.

ASSESSING STRATEGY USE

Each module offers a plethora of practice activities. As students are practicing, you can observe and assess the extent to which they are able to apply the selected strategy. **Observation tools** help you keep track of where each student is and monitor their progress. An observation tool can be simple, such as a class list with an extra column. Your observations can be codes:

+ Is regularly implementing the strategy adeptly

✔ Understands the strategy, takes time to think it through

– Is not implementing the strategy accurately

A note-taking observation tool provides space for you to insert notes about how a student is doing (see Figure 13). You can laminate the tool and use dry-erase markers to reuse it for different observations, use sticky notes, or just write in the boxes.

FIGURE 13 ● Example Note-Taking Observation Tool

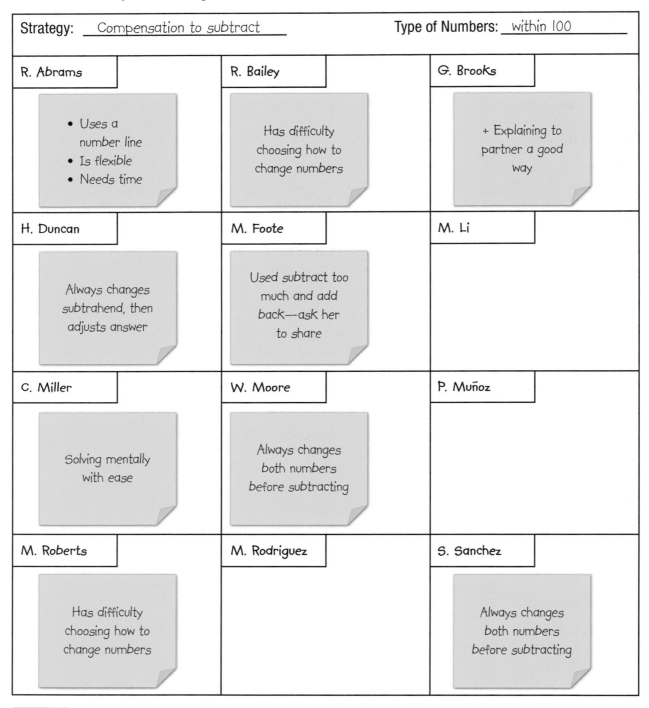

Strategy: __Compensation to subtract__   Type of Numbers: __within 100__

R. Abrams	R. Bailey	G. Brooks
• Uses a number line • Is flexible • Needs time	Has difficulty choosing how to change numbers	+ Explaining to partner a good way
H. Duncan	M. Foote	M. Li
Always changes subtrahend, then adjusts answer	Used subtract too much and add back—ask her to share	
C. Miller	W. Moore	P. Muñoz
Solving mentally with ease	Always changes both numbers before subtracting	
M. Roberts	M. Rodriguez	S. Sanchez
Has difficulty choosing how to change numbers		Always changes both numbers before subtracting

Some days, you collect data on some students; other days, you collect data on other students. The data can help in classroom discussions and in planning for instructional next steps.

Journal prompts provide an opportunity for students to write about their thinking process. Each module provides a collection of prompts that you might use for journaling. You can modify those or easily craft your own. The prompt can specifically ask students to explain how they used the strategy:

> Explain and show how you can use Make Hundreds to solve this problem: 637 + 693

Or a prompt can focus on identifying when that strategy is a good idea:

> Circle the problems that are good choices for solving with the Make Hundreds strategy and tell why you selected them:
>
> 495 + 347   327 + 726   489 + 278   399 + 298

Interviewing is an excellent way to really understand student thinking. You can pick any problem that lends to the strategy you are working on and write it on a note card (or record two or three on separate notecards). While students are engaged in an instructional or practice activity, roam the room, select a child, show them a card, and ask them (1) to solve it and (2) explain how they thought about it. You can pair this with an observation tool to keep track of how each student is progressing.

HOW DO I USE PART 3 TO SUPPORT STUDENTS' FLUENCY?

As soon as students know more than one way, it is time to integrate routines, tasks, centers, and games that focus on choosing when to use a strategy. That is where Part 3 comes in. As you read in Fluency Action 1, students need to be able to choose efficient strategies. The strategy modules provide students *access* to those strategies, ensuring the strategies make sense and giving students ample opportunities to practice those strategies and become adept at using them. However, if you stop there, students are left on their own when it comes to choosing which strategy to use when. It is like having a set of knives in the kitchen but not knowing which ones to use for slicing cheese or bread, cutting meat, or chopping vegetables. Like with food, some items can be cut with various knives, but other food really needs a specific knife.

Do not wait until after all strategies are learned to focus on when to use a strategy—instead weave in Part 3 activities regularly. Each time a new strategy is learned, it is time to revisit activities that engage students in making choices from among the strategies in their repertoire. Students must learn what to look for in a problem to decide which strategy they will use to solve the problem *efficiently* based on the numbers in the problem. This is *flexibility* in action, and thus leads to fluency.

IN SUM, MAKING A DIFFERENCE

Part 1 has briefly described factors that are important in developing fluency, and these ideas are important as you implement activities from the modules. We sum up Part 1 with the following five key takeaways:

1. Be clear on what fluency means (three components and six actions). This includes communicating it to students and their parents.

2. Attend to readiness skills: conceptual understanding, properties, utilities, computational estimation, and, of course, basic fact fluency.

3. Through activities and discussion, help students connect on the features of a problem and how that relates to good strategy options.

4. Reinforce student reasoning and choice selection, rather than focus on speed and accuracy. Getting the strategies down initially takes more time but eventually will become more efficient.

TEACHING TAKEAWAY

Teaching for fluency means teaching strategies as core instruction, routinely practicing them, and offering opportunities for students to choose among strategies.

5. Assess fluency, not just accuracy.

Time invested in strategy work has big payoffs—confident and fluent students! That is why we have so many activities in this book. Teach the strategies as part of core instruction, *and* continue to practice throughout the year, looping back to strategies that students might be forgetting to use (with Part 2 activities) and offering ongoing opportunities to choose from among strategies (with Part 3 activities).

PART 2

STRATEGY MODULES

Count On/Count Back Strategy

STRATEGY OVERVIEW:
Count On/Count Back

What is Count On? The Count On strategy begins with single digits (i.e., basic facts), counting on from one addend. For example, to add 8 + 5, start with 8 and count on 5 more. Count On extends this idea, using flexible skip counting to efficiently determine a sum. You start with either addend and add on the other number using convenient chunks.

What is Count Back? The Count Back strategy also begins with single-digit problems, such as 9 – 4, where students start at 9 and count back 4. Count Back is used for subtraction in both "separate" (take away from the minuend) and "compare" (difference between the minuend and the subtrahend) problem situations. This module focuses on "separate" and Module 5 (Think Addition) focuses on "compare."

HOW DOES COUNT ON/COUNT BACK WORK?

Students choose benchmark numbers and keep track of partial results as they go. They may keep track in writing or mentally. In either case, they may use a series of equations or a number line to keep track. At first, students tend to use more steps (counts), but with experience, the chunks become more efficient. Flexibility is key.

COUNT ON OPTIONS USING AN OPEN NUMBER LINE

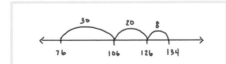 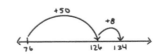 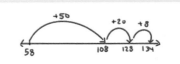

COUNT ON OPTIONS FOR 58 + 76 USING EQUATIONS

76 + 30 = 106	76 + 50 = 126	58 + 50 = 108
106 + 20 = 126	126 + 8 = 134	108 + 20 = 128
126 + 8 = 134		128 + 6 = 134

COUNT BACK OPTIONS USING AN OPEN NUMBER LINE

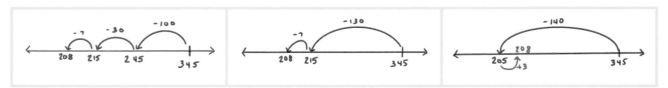

COUNT BACK OPTIONS FOR 345 – 137 USING EQUATIONS

345 – 100 = 245	345 – 130 = 215	345 – 140 = 205
245 – 30 = 215	215 – 7 = 208	205 + 3 = 208
215 – 7 = 208		[blends with Compensation]

WHEN DO YOU CHOOSE COUNT ON/COUNT BACK?

When one of the addends is relatively small, Count On is an efficient strategy (e.g., 4,579 + 215). Count Back is useful when the number being subtracted (subtrahend) is small. However, when a subtraction problem has a subtrahend close to the minuend (e.g., 436 – 385), a Think Addition or Count Up method is often more efficient.

COUNT ON AND COUNT BACK:
Strategy Briefs for Families

It is important that families understand the strategies and know how they work so that they can be partners in the pursuit of fluency. These strategy briefs are a tool for doing that. You can include them in parent or school newsletters or share them at parent conferences. They are available for download so that you can adjust them as needed.

Count On Strategy

How It Works: To add, we can break apart an addend and count on from the other addend in chunks.

1. Choose which addend to break apart and which to count on from.
2. Break apart the addend into easy chunks.
3. Count on using the chunks you chose.

The left example shows that you can break apart 58 and count on from 76.

The right example shows that you can also break apart 76 and count on from 58.

When It's Useful: Count On is useful when you can easily break apart one of the addends into convenient chunks. These addends are typically small (two, three, or four digits).

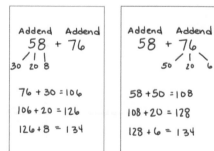

Count Back Strategy

How It Works: To subtract, we can break apart the subtrahend (second number) and count back from the minuend (first number).

1. Break apart the subtrahend (the second number) into easy chunks.
2. Count back from the minuend (the first number) by the chunks.
3. The last count is the answer.

The left example shows how 137 can be broken into 100, 30, and 7. Note that those chunks can be counted in any order.

The right example shows how the person counts back 25 first and then 400.

When It's Useful: Count Back is useful when the number being subtracted is small. Count Back is also useful when the difference between the two numbers is small.

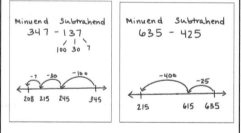

These resources can be downloaded at **resources.corwin.com/FOF/addsubtractwholenumber**.

MODULE 1 Count On/ Count Back

MODULE 2 Make Tens

MODULE 3 Count On/ Count Back

MODULE 4 Count On/ Count Back

MODULE 5 Count On/ Count Back

MODULE 6 Count On/ Count Back

TEACHING ACTIVITIES for Count On/ Count Back

Count On and Count Back are often the first strategies students learn. What begins as count on or back by ones becomes count on by tens and then larger chunks like 30 or 100. In this section, you'll find instructional activities for helping students develop efficient ways to count on or count back. The goal is that students become adept at using counting strategies efficiently and accurately and also consider when they will want to use a counting strategy.

ACTIVITY 1.1
CONNECTING REPRESENTATIONS WHEN COUNTING ON

Count On is a strategy for finding the sum when addition is being used. One way to develop this understanding, and to model it, is to represent it with base-10 blocks, place value disks, and number lines. In this activity, have students show Count On with math tools such as place value disks or base-10 blocks. They record adding chunks on a number line or set of equations. The following image shows what this would look like for 132 + 45.

Students use place value disks to solve the problem.

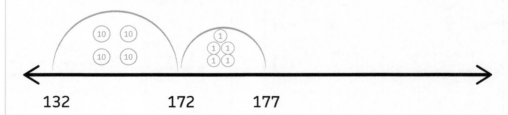

Students later transition to chunking place value disks. They work toward using the least amount of chunks, making it a more efficient strategy.

ACTIVITY 1.2
CONNECTING REPRESENTATIONS WHEN COUNTING BACK

Count Back is a strategy for finding the difference when subtraction is being used to take away. A good way to develop this understanding, and to model it, is to represent it with base-10 blocks and number lines. In this activity, have students show Count Back with base-10 blocks and record taking away chunks on a number line or set of equations. The following image shows what this would look like for 245 – 132.

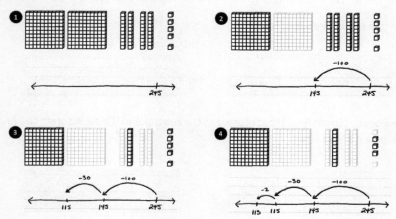

Be sure that students record each jump as they take away a certain amount. You also want students to record the equation that goes with the work. For step 2, the student would write 245 – 100 = 145. For step 3, the recording would be 145 – 30 = 115. The last recording would be 115 – 3 = 112. After students complete the problem, facilitate a discussion about the differences in how students counted back.

ACTIVITY 1.3
BEADED NUMBER LINES

One way to develop the understanding of Count On and Count Back is to represent it with a 100 beaded number line and connect the work to a written number line. In this activity, students partition the beads to represent the first addend. Then students would shift beads to count on the amount of the second addend. This creates the sum. Students then record their work on a number line. Consider 45 + 17. Students move 45 beads to the left.

> **TEACHING TAKEAWAY**
> It can be helpful for students to use clothespins to keep the amount they're working with separate from the unused beads.

Then, students count on 17 more before counting a total.

(Continued)

(Continued)

After using the bead counters, students record their thinking on a bead counter recording sheet.

To count back, students slide 45 beads to the left to represent the minuend. A clothespin is handy here for keeping the minuend separate from the rest of the beads. The following example shows how this would unfold with 45 – 17.

Students separate 45 from the entire set of beads.

Then, students shift the beads (Count Back) that represent the subtrahend. This will create the final difference. Students then record their work on a number line.

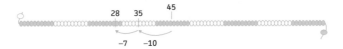

After completing the work, students record their thinking on a bead counter number line.

RESOURCE(S) FOR THIS ACTIVITY

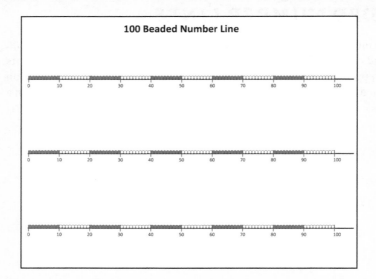

100 Beaded Number Line

online resources ⌐ This resource can be downloaded at **resources.corwin.com/FOF/addsubtractwholenumber**.

ACTIVITY 1.4
NUMBER BONDS FOR COUNT ON/COUNT BACK IN CHUNKS

Number bonds let students decompose numbers in useful ways. Students use the number bond to help them decompose a number into convenient parts. In the Count On version, after a problem is posed, students first determine which addend to count on from and which addend to break apart. Then students count on using the number line and the decomposed parts. In Count On example 58 + 36, a student thinks to break apart 36 into 3 tens, 5 ones, and another one and then shows those jumps on the number line. This activity also works well to develop the Count Back strategy. Students decompose the subtrahend and then count back from the minuend.

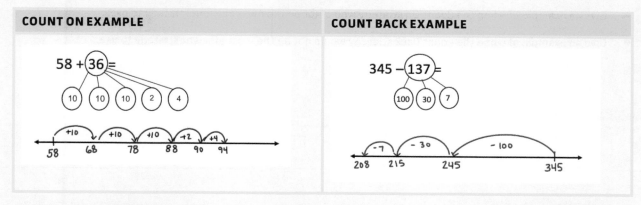

As students decompose numbers, look for them to break a number in each 10 or chunks of 10. In Count Back example 345 – 137, the student makes a jump of 30 instead of three jumps of 10. You want to help students move from individual hundreds, tens, or ones to groups of each.

ACTIVITY 1.5
PROMPTS FOR TEACHING COUNT ON/ COUNT BACK

Use the following prompts as opportunities to develop understanding of and reasoning with the strategy. Have students use representations and tools to justify their thinking including base-10 models, number lines, number charts, and so on. After students work with the prompt(s), bring the class together to exchange ideas. These could be useful for collecting evidence of student understanding. Any prompt can be easily modified to feature different numbers (e.g., three-digit or four-digit numbers) and any prompt can be offered more than once if modified.

- Show two different ways to add 35 + 76 using a number line. Do they have the same sum? Explain your thinking.

- Andie counts on to solve 496 + 237. What number would you suggest she start with? How should she then count on from the number you suggest? Show your thinking with a number line or equations.

- Show two different ways to subtract 376 – 135 using a number line. Do they have the same difference? Explain your answer.

- Siobhan counts back to solve 705 – 183. What jump would you suggest Siobhan start with? How should she then count back from the number you suggest? Show your thinking with a number line or equations.

(Continued)

(*Continued*)

- Create a problem that you would solve by counting back. Show how you can use the Count Back strategy to solve your problem.

- Create a problem that you would solve by counting on. Show how you can use the Count On strategy to solve your problem.

- Emma solved 516 + 475 by thinking 516 + 100 + 100 + 100 + 100 + 10 + 10 + 10 + 10 + 10 + 10 + 10 + 1 + 1 + 1 + 1 + 1. What is another way she might have thought about the problem?

- How are Count On and Count Back similar and how are they different?

- Give an example of when the Count On strategy would not be the most efficient strategy to use.

- Give an example of when the Count Back strategy would not be the most efficient strategy to use.

NOTES

_____

_____

_____

_____

_____

_____

_____

_____

_____

_____

PRACTICE ACTIVITIES for Count On/Count Back

Fluency is realized through quality practice that is focused, varied, processed, and connected. The activities in this section focus students' attention on how this strategy works and when to use it. The activities are a collection of varied engagements. The discussion you facilitate after an activity or the reflection prompts you attach to it should help students think about what they did mathematically, how they reasoned about the activity, and when the math they did (namely the strategy) might be useful. Debriefing should also help students see how the practice activity connects to recent instruction or how the strategy connects to other strategies they know. Game boards, recording sheets, digit cards, and other required materials are available as online resources for you to download, possibly modify, and use. As students work with activities, you want to look for how well they are acquiring the strategy and assimilating it into their collection of strategies.

FLUENCY COMPONENT	WHAT TO LOOK FOR AS STUDENTS PRACTICE THIS STRATEGY
Efficiency	• Are students using the Count On/Count Back strategy efficiently? (e.g., Are they counting efficiently?) • Do they use the strategy regardless of its appropriateness for the problem at hand? (e.g., Do they count by ones when one addend is a multiple of 10, like 40?) • Do they change their approach to or from this strategy as they begin to work the problem and realize the initial approach will be less efficient?
Flexibility	• Are students using the Count On/Count Back strategy in groups or singles? • Are students counting in appropriate ways or do they rely on the same (usually lower-level) counting approach? • Are students carrying out the strategy in flexible ways? (e.g., Do they sensibly choose what number to count on from?) • Do they change their counting approach if it doesn't seem to be working?
Accuracy	• Are students using the Count On/Count Back strategy accurately? • Are students accurate with certain counts (e.g., counting by groups of 10, counting around a decade or century)? • Are students finding accurate solutions? • Are they considering the reasonableness of their solutions?* • How is estimation worked into the practice?*

*This consideration is not unique to this strategy and should be practiced throughout the pursuit of fluency with whole numbers.

WORKED EXAMPLES

Worked examples are problems that have been solved. Correctly worked examples can help students make sense of a strategy and incorrectly worked examples attend to common errors.

Related to the Count On/Count Back strategy, worked examples can help students see different options for skip counting and help them work toward efficient ways to count on or back. Incorrectly worked examples are based on common challenges or errors when using counting strategies, as seen in the following examples:

1. The student loses track of how many jumps and makes too many or too few jumps.

    • 871 – 355: counts back 771, 661, 551, 441, then continues jumps for tens and ones.

    • 394 + 477: starts at 400 and counts on to 877 but forgets to count back 6.

2. The student makes an error in breaking apart a number.
   - 87 + 71: from 87, counts on 20 to get to 107 and then 40 [rather than 50] to get to 147 and one more to 148.
   - 4,225 − 1,270: counts back 1,200 to 3,025, then back 25 to 3,000, then back 55 [rather than 45] to 2,945.
3. The student misses a count when consecutive digits are the same.
   - 871 − 449: counts back 4 hundreds to 471 but overlooks 4 tens because a jump of 4 was just made.

Although not an error, students may continue to count by single ones, tens, or hundreds instead of counting in chunks or multiples of these. Show a worked example that does this and ask students to consider how they might combine jumps to add/subtract more efficiently. Various worked examples can be found throughout this module, or you can collect authentic worked examples (see prompts from Activity 1.5, for example). Additionally, have students compare worked examples to highlight different ways to count on or back. A sampling of ideas are provided in the following table.

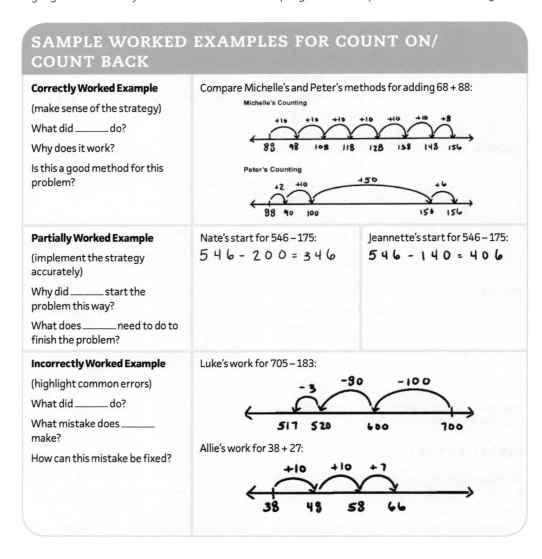

SAMPLE WORKED EXAMPLES FOR COUNT ON/ COUNT BACK

Correctly Worked Example (make sense of the strategy) What did _____ do? Why does it work? Is this a good method for this problem?	Compare Michelle's and Peter's methods for adding 68 + 88: Michelle's Counting +10 +10 +10 +10 +10 +10 +8 88 98 108 118 128 138 148 156 Peter's Counting +2 +10 +50 +6 88 90 100 150 156
Partially Worked Example (implement the strategy accurately) Why did _____ start the problem this way? What does _____ need to do to finish the problem?	Nate's start for 546 − 175: $546 - 200 = 346$ Jeannette's start for 546 − 175: $546 - 140 = 406$
Incorrectly Worked Example (highlight common errors) What did _____ do? What mistake does _____ make? How can this mistake be fixed?	Luke's work for 705 − 183: −3 −80 −100 517 520 600 700 Allie's work for 38 + 27: +10 +10 +7 38 48 58 66

ACTIVITY 1.6

Name: "Or You Could"
Type: Routine

About the Routine: Count On is most efficient when done in chunks. Students may be comfortable counting on by ones, tens, or hundreds instead of groups. This routine helps students work to use chunks by renaming expressions that add singles as expressions that add groups. In it, students are shown a basic (inefficient) approach to count on or count back. It asks them to think of another way they could carry out the strategy. Keep in mind that it is reasonable for students to first learn and use Count On and Count Back by decomposing a number into individual tens and ones and counting by each. The strategy is most efficiently used by counting on or back by chunks. This routine helps students develop more efficient approaches for counting.

Materials: list of two or three completed examples of Count On or Count Back

Directions:
1. Provide completed Count On or Count Back problems such as the following examples.

   • You can solve 26 + 45 by thinking 26 + 10 + 10 + 10 + 10 + 1 + 1 + 1 + 1 + 1 or you could …

   • You can solve 92 – 64 by thinking 92 – 10 – 10 – 10 – 10 – 10 – 10 – 1 – 1 – 1 – 1 or you could …

   • You can solve 516 + 145 by thinking 516 + 100 + 10 + 10 + 10 + 10 + 1 + 1 + 1 + 1 + 1 or you could …

   • You could solve 421 – 233 by thinking 400 – 100 – 100 – 10 – 10 – 10 – 1 – 1 – 1 or you could …

2. Ask students to talk with a partner about another way to count on or back.

3. After a few moments, bring the group together to share their thinking.

4. As students share more efficient ways to chunk the skip counts, record their thinking on a number line or with an equation.

5. Reinforce to students how the different approaches yield the same sum or difference.

To note, it's important to avoid using too many approaches. You want students to find and explain efficient approaches. In time, you can begin to modify the routine even further by providing a slightly more efficient chunking as shown in these two examples. Even though the hundreds were chunked, there is still an opportunity to chunk the tens and ones.

• You could solve 716 + 244 by thinking 716 + 200 + 10 + 10 + 10 + 10 + 4 or you could …

• You could solve 91 – 33 by thinking 91 – 1 – 10 – 10 – 10 – 2 or you could …

Keep in mind that sometimes chunking may be manipulated for friendlier computations. For example, in 378 + 344, one might add on 300 (678), then 2 (680), then 20 (700) to make a 10 and then a 100 and last add the remaining 22 (722). No matter how students think about chunking addends or subtrahends for Count On or Count Back, be sure to ask them to explain why that approach is efficient. Also, be sure that you accept their thinking and share other ideas but be careful to avoid saying that one way is "correct."

TEACHING TAKEAWAY

Ask students to explain why an approach is efficient but avoid saying one way is correct.

ACTIVITY 1.7

Name: "The Count"　　　　　　　　**Type:** Routine

About the Routine: This routine has students estimate and skip count. It is a good opportunity for practicing skip counting by a variety of intervals, which is essential for using the Count On and Count Back strategies.

Materials: Identify a counting interval and a starting number, provide a supporting number chart.

Directions:

1. Set a clear counting path so that students know how they will count in the room. Having students gather in a large circle is a good option.

2. Identify a starting number, the student who will count first, and a counting interval such as skip count forward by tens. Then, ask students about the impending count. Here are some questions to ask:

   · What are some numbers we will say as we count?

   · What number do you think you will say?

   · What will be the last number said?

3. As students count, you can record the numbers they say on the board or mark them on a related number chart or number line. Doing either will help a postcount discussion about the patterns within the numbers that were said and discussion about the predictions made before the count.

4. After the count, discuss patterns within the numbers said, challenges with counting, and how student predictions compared with the results of the count.

THE COUNT			
Start with 108.	Start with 336.	Start with 517.	Start with 784.
Count on by 20.	Count on by 50.	Count back by 10.	Count back by 5.

The example shows a variety of prompts you can pose. Note that counting backward is also an important use of the routine because it aligns with subtraction. Also note that there are a variety of intervals provided. Students should have experience working with a variety of skip counts to help them move from counting by singles to groups.

ACTIVITY 1.8

Name: "Strategize First Jumps"   **Type:** Routine

About the Routine: This routine helps students consider different ways to skip count in order to efficiently solve a problem. It helps students think strategically about decomposing problems.

Materials: list of three to four problems on the same topic but that lend to different ways to count on/count back

Directions: This routine involves showing a series of problems, one at a time, like a Number Talk (Parrish, 2014).

1. Ask students to mentally determine their first jump (only), and signal when ready (since it is only the first jump, they only need about 10–15 seconds).

2. Ask different students to share what they would do as their first jump. Record all ideas using a number line or Hundred Chart.

3. Ask students to pick one of the first jump ideas and finish the problem.

4. Share answers and discuss whether the first jump they chose worked out well or not.

5. Repeat with other problems (as time allows).

6. Conclude the series with a synthesizing discussion, asking questions such as these: What are efficient ways to count on (count back)? When will you use a Count On or Count Back strategy? When might counting not work very well?

This routine can also focus *only* on first jumps (without finishing the problems). Then, more examples can be used in less time. Possible problems to use include the following:

48 + 25	91 + 329	632 + 754	2,560 + 1,576
15 + 17	42 + 235	482 + 258	7,279 + 5,301
29 − 18	734 − 36	328 − 284	4,274 − 4,525
63 − 12	551 − 71	537 − 335	6,533 − 3,717

RESOURCE(S) FOR THIS ACTIVITY

48 + 25	15 + 17
91 + 329	42 + 235
632 + 754	482 + 258
2,560 + 1,576	7,279 + 5,301
472 + 85	945 + 74

29 − 18	63 − 12
551 − 71	734 − 36
328 − 284	537 − 335
4,274 − 4,525	6,533 − 3,717
724 − 48	957 − 804

 These game cards can be downloaded at **resources.corwin.com/FOF/addsubtractwholenumber**.

ACTIVITY 1.9

Name: *Count On Bingo*   **Type:** *Game*

About the Game: *Count On Bingo* helps students think about the jumps they make and how they might become more strategic with their jumps. Blank 5 × 5 bingo boards can be downloaded and students can then create their own boards by writing the numbers 1–9 and multiples of 10 randomly anywhere on their board.

Materials: *Count On Bingo* boards (one per student), counters, expression cards (or a list of expressions)

Directions: 1. Players take turns pulling expression cards.

2. Players solve the expression on the card using the Count On strategy.

3. Then players place a counter on the jumps/chunks they used to solve their expression.

4. Bingo is five counters in a row in any direction.

For example, students pull the expression card 48 + 23. Player 1's jumps are 10 + 10 + 3 (on the left board) and they put two counters on the 10 and one counter on the 3. Player 2's jumps are 20 + 3 (on the right board) and they place a counter on those numbers. Note that player 1 stacked the counters on the 10 for this problem because they made two jumps of 10.

<table>
<tr><td colspan="5" align="center">Count On Bingo</td><td colspan="5" align="center">Count On Bingo</td></tr>
<tr><td colspan="5">Directions: Choose from the numbers in the box. Write a number in each box. You can write a number more than once.</td><td colspan="5">Directions: Choose from the numbers in the box. Write a number in each box. You can write a number more than once.</td></tr>
<tr><td colspan="5">0 1 2 3 4 5 6 7 8 9 10 20 30 40 50 60 70 80 90</td><td colspan="5">0 1 2 3 4 5 6 7 8 9 10 20 30 40 50 60 70 80 90</td></tr>
<tr><td>(10)</td><td>4</td><td>30</td><td>20</td><td>10</td><td>40</td><td>3</td><td>20</td><td>10</td><td>50</td></tr>
<tr><td>6</td><td>10</td><td>40</td><td>10</td><td>(3)</td><td>8</td><td>10</td><td>(3)</td><td>1</td><td>20</td></tr>
<tr><td>70</td><td>2</td><td>90</td><td>5</td><td>30</td><td>7</td><td>10</td><td>(20)</td><td>30</td><td>40</td></tr>
<tr><td>6</td><td>20</td><td>7</td><td>70</td><td>80</td><td>6</td><td>5</td><td>70</td><td>6</td><td>8</td></tr>
<tr><td>10</td><td>10</td><td>1</td><td>8</td><td>40</td><td>1</td><td>10</td><td>10</td><td>90</td><td>4</td></tr>
</table>

You can find a list of expressions at the companion website that might be used for playing the game, although it will work with any examples. Expressions can be written on index cards if you want small groups of students to play *Count On Bingo* without you.

online resources Game cards and this game board can be downloaded at **resources.corwin.com/FOF/ addsubtractwholenumber**.

ACTIVITY 1.10

Name: *Pick Your Jumps*   **Type:** *Game*

About the Game: *Pick Your Jumps* helps students choose the most efficient amount of jumps. Players win each round by solving a problem accurately with the fewest jumps.

Materials: a short list of expressions or expressions recorded on index cards, *Pick Your Jumps* game board

Directions:
1. Players take turns pulling expression cards and solving the problem with a Count On or Count Back strategy.

2. Players solve the problem and record the number of jumps they made.

3. The player with the fewest number of jumps gets a point for the round. Note that the solution must be correct to earn a point.

4. The player with the most points at the end of four rounds wins.

For example, players turn over 21 + 46. Player 1 solves it by counting on from 21 by 10s (4 jumps) and jumping 6 (1 jump) to reach 67. Player 2 solves it by counting on from 46 by 10s (2 jumps) and jumping 6 (1 jump) to equal 67. Player 2 scores a point.

RESOURCE(S) FOR THIS ACTIVITY

21 + 46	31 + 17
41 + 31	52 + 34
55 + 38	39 + 42
53 + 18	44 + 37
98 + 56	87 + 45

183 + 355	880 + 114
339 + 140	135 + 543
514 + 399	682 + 170
140 + 267	539 + 370
483 + 452	930 + 113

50 − 44	51 − 30
100 − 49	64 − 45
30 − 12	94 − 56
543 − 240	85 − 47
444 − 78	96 − 44

444 − 393	672 − 305
281 − 113	577 − 145
904 − 236	474 − 169
616 − 377	501 − 188
229 − 192	990 − 538

Pick Your Jumps

online resources — Game cards and this game board can be downloaded at **resources.corwin.com/FOF/ addsubtractwholenumber**.

ACTIVITY 1.11

Name: Make It Close   **Type:** Game

About the Game: *Make It Close* is a target-based game for practicing addition and developing number sense. The goal is to create a sum as close to the target as possible. The unique twist in this game is that the target changes from round to round.

Materials: four decks of digit cards (0–9) or playing cards (with aces equal to 1; face cards and 10s removed), *Make It Close* recording sheet

Directions:

1. Players deal four cards to make 2 two-digit addends. Both players use the Count On strategy to find the sum, which becomes the target for the round. In the example, the target for round 1 is 103.

2. Each player deals themselves four digit cards to make an addition problem with 2 two-digit addends.

3. The players arrange the four digits so that their sum is close to the target. For example, player 1 arranges digits for a sum of 109. Player 2 arranges digits for a product of 101.

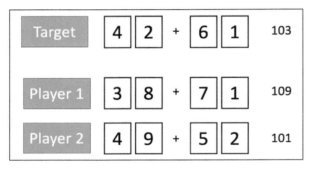

4. The player with the sum closest to the target for round 1 gets a point. This is player 2 in the example.

5. The first player to earn 5 points wins the game.

> **TEACHING TAKEAWAY**
> Have students say aloud to their partner how they counted on to add.

RESOURCE(S) FOR THIS ACTIVITY

Make It Close

Directions: Use digit cards to make an addition problem. The sum of the problem is the target. Deal new digit cards to make an addition problem that is close to the target. The player closest to the target gets a point.

Target Problem	My Problem
	(give yourself a √ if you are closest to the target)

ACTIVITY 1.12

Name: Find the Equation   **Type:** Center

About the Center: This center helps students think about how they can count on or back. It also connects representations of number lines and equations. While described as a center, Find the Equation can also be used as an instructional activity.

Materials: open number line cards, Find the Equation recording sheet (one per student)

Directions: 1. Students select a number line card.

2. Students generate values for each jump and record the equation that the number line card might model.

3. Students repeat step 2 to show a different problem with the same number line card to show another problem it might model.

For example, a student picks the number line card shown.

	Student thinks of each jump as a jump of 10 and records:	Student records the equation:
? 444	$444 - 10 = 434$ $434 - 10 = 424$ $424 - 10 = 414$ $414 - 10 = 404$	$444 - 40 = 404$
? 444	Student thinks of each jump as 2 jumps of 100 and 2 tens: $444 - 100 = 244$ $344 - 100 = 244$ $244 - 10 = 234$ $234 - 10 = 224$	Student records the equation: $444 - 220 = 224$

RESOURCE(S) FOR THIS ACTIVITY

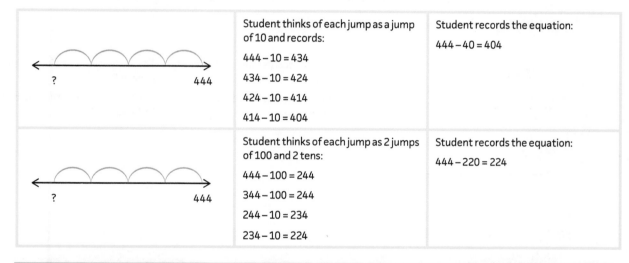

Number line cards and this recording sheet can be downloaded at **resources.corwin.com/FOF/ addsubtractwholenumber**.

online
resources

ACTIVITY 1.13

Name: Same But Different   **Type:** Center

About the Center: This center helps students recognize that numbers can be added in different ways and to develop efficiency when counting on or counting back by connecting single counts to group counts.

Materials: open number line cards, Same But Different recording sheet

Directions: 1. Students select an open number line card.

2. Students copy the image and record the value of jumps shown on the number line and the equation.

3. Students record the jumps on the related number line with jumps that represent chunks of ones, tens, or hundreds.

4. After working with the center, students should be asked to explain how the problems are the same and how they are different.

The following is an example.

| 553 + 48 | The student records 4 jumps of 10 and a jump of 8.

 The student records the equation 553 + 48 = 601. | The student records a jump of 40 and a jump of 8.

 The student records the equation 553 + 48 = 601. |

RESOURCE(S) FOR THIS ACTIVITY

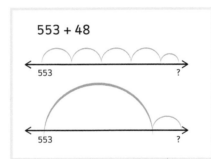

online resources — Number line cards and this recording sheet can be downloaded at **resources.corwin.com/FOF/ addsubtractwholenumber**.

ACTIVITY 1.14

Name: The Largest Sum, The Smallest Sum **Type:** Center

About the Center: This center reinforces Count On or Count Back strategies while also focusing on number sense and reasoning. It can be used as a game where students earn points for finding the largest or smallest sum within a group.

Materials: digit cards (0–9) or playing cards (queens = 0, aces = 1, kings and jacks removed); The Largest Sum, The Smallest Sum recording sheet

Directions:
1. Students pull three digit cards to make a three-digit number.

2. Students then pull three additional digit cards to make a second three-digit number.

3. Students arrange the digits in each addend to make the largest sum.

4. Students record the problem and use Count On to find the sum.

5. Students repeat the activity but this time, they rearrange the digits in each addend to make the smallest sum once again use Count On to find the sum.

6. Students record their thinking on the recording sheet or in their journals.

RESOURCE(S) FOR THIS ACTIVITY

The Largest Sum, The Smallest Sum

Directions: Pull three digit cards to make a number. Pull three digit cards to make another number. Arrange the digits in each number to make the largest sum. Count on to show the sum. Then, rearrange the digits in each number to make the smallest sum.

Largest Sum		Smallest Sum	
First Addend:	Second Addend:	First Addend:	Second Addend:
Show how you added		Show how you added	
Sum:		Sum:	

1	2	3	4
5	6	7	8
9	1	2	3
4	5	6	7
8	9	0	0

online resources Digit cards and this recording sheet can be downloaded at **resources.corwin.com/ FOF/addsubtractwholenumber**.

Make Tens Strategy

STRATEGY OVERVIEW:
Make Tens

What is Make Tens? This strategy begins with basic facts as the Making 10 strategy, which involves decomposing one of the addends to make a 10 with the other. It can be represented in various ways.

$$8 + 5 = 10 + 3 \qquad 58 + 5 = 60 + 3$$

Make Tens is one of the most adaptable and useful reasoning strategies. Extended to multidigit addition, the strategy involves making tens, hundreds, or thousands by moving a quantity from one addend to another.

HOW DOES MAKE TENS WORK?

Grounded in place value and the properties, this strategy involves breaking apart (decomposing) one of the addends and associating it with another addend with the intent of making tens, hundreds, or thousands. Put simply, it looks like this:

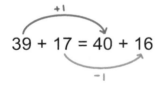 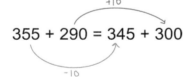 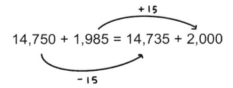

$$39 + 17 = 40 + 16 \qquad 355 + 290 = 345 + 300 \qquad 14{,}750 + 1{,}985 = 14{,}735 + 2{,}000$$

TEACHING TAKEAWAY

Writing down addends can help students track their thinking, eventually moving toward using a mental process.

Note that in the first example, the equation could have also been changed by giving 3 to 17, creating the expression 36 + 20. In these examples, the move involved going *up* to the benchmark. The strategy also works for going *down* to a benchmark.

Make Tens is considered a mental process, but it doesn't have to be. As numbers get larger, students may wish to write down their adjusted addends so they don't have to keep it all in their head. Even with writing the newly formed expression, the process can be more efficient and accurate than the standard algorithm because it does not require regrouping.

WHEN DO YOU CHOOSE MAKE TENS?

Make Tens works when at least one of the addends is close to a benchmark. It works with any number of addends. With more addends come more options of how to make tens. What ways do you see for 17 + 25 + 19 + 26? Conversely, Make Tens may not be an efficient strategy when it is difficult to make tens, hundreds, or thousands. For example, making 400 for 658 + 377 involves adding 23 to 658, which is a more involved addition expression.

MAKE TENS:
Strategy Briefs for Families

It is important that families understand the strategies and know how they work so that they can be partners in the pursuit of fluency. These strategy briefs are a tool for doing that. You can include them in parent or school newsletters or share them at parent conferences. They are available for download so that you can adjust them as needed.

Make Tens Strategy

How It Works: We can break apart one addend and give some to another addend to make a 10.

1. Choose which addend you find easy to make into the next 10.
2. Break apart the other addend. Give some of that number to the other number.
3. The other number will now make a 10.
4. Add the parts together.

In the left example, 39 is close to 40. To make it a 40, you break apart 17 into 1 and 16. Use 1 and add it to the 39 to make 40. Now add the 16 you have left to the 40. 39 + 17 becomes 40 + 16.

In the right example, 58 is close to 60. To make 60, you take 2 from the 6. Then add that to the 58. The new number sentence is 60 + 4. 60 + 4 = 64

When It's Useful: Make Tens is useful when adding 2 two-digit addends or a two-digit addend and a one-digit addend. Remember that either addend can be made into the next 10.

Addend Addend	Addend Addend
39 + 17	58 + 6
39 + 17 (+1) ↓ ↓ (-1)	58 + 6 (+2) ↓ ↓ (-2)
40 16	60 4
40 + 16 = 56 (sum)	60 + 4 = 64 (sum)

Make Hundreds Strategy

How It Works: We can break apart one addend and give some to another addend to make a hundred.

1. Choose which addend you find easy to make into the next hundred.
2. Break apart the other addend. Give some of that number to the other number.
3. The other number will now make a hundred.
4. Add the parts together.

When It's Useful: Make Hundreds is useful when you can easily determine what the next hundred is for one of the addends. It can also be used with make a thousand.

Addend Addend	Addend Addend
355 + 290	14,750 + 1,985
355 + 290 (-10) ↓ ↓ (+10)	14,750 + 1,985 (-15) ↓ ↓ (+15)
345 300	14,735 2,000
345 + 300 = 645 (sum)	14,735 + 2,000 = 16,735 (sum)

online resources 🔍 These resources can be downloaded at **resources.corwin.com/FOF/ addsubtractwholenumber**.

NOTES

_____

_____

_____

_____

MODULE 1 Count On/Count Back

MODULE 2 Make Tens Strategy

MODULE 3 Partial Sums and Differences Strategy

MODULE 4 Compensation Strategy

MODULE 5 Think Addition Strategy

MODULE 6 Standard Algorithms for Addition and Subtraction

TEACHING ACTIVITIES for Make Tens

Before students are able to choose strategies, a key to fluency, they first must be able to understand and use relevant strategies. These activities focus specifically on Make Tens (and Hundreds and Thousands). While students may employ other methods, which is appropriate, they also must learn this important strategy that employs and strengthens their place value understanding and flexible use of properties.

ACTIVITY 2.1
CONNECTING TRAINS

Have students build a stick of nine Unifix Cubes (all one color) and another stick of five cubes (all of a different color). Ask students to predict how many there will be if they combine the two sticks. Discuss how one cube can be moved to the stick of nine to make a 10. Talk about how making a 10 helps students find the total.

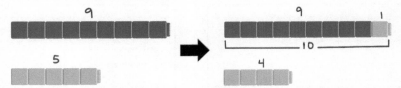

Repeat the activity with a variety of stick combinations such as 9 and 7, 6 and 8, or 8 and 3. Focus students' attention on the action of making a 10 and having some more. For two-digit addends, students will need to make sticks of 10. The following chart shows some numbers to consider. Again, each time be sure to focus on making a new 10.

9 + 5	19 + 5	29 + 5	39 + 5
9 + 7	19 + 7	29 + 7	39 + 7
6 + 8	6 + 18	6 + 28	6 + 38

Progress to working with 2 two-digit addends. The following chart shows some expressions you might use. Represent each addend with Unifix cubes and have students show the movement of the units.

7 + 5	17 + 15	17 + 25	17 + 55
8 + 6	18 + 16	28 + 26	48 + 26
4 + 9	14 + 19	34 + 39	64 + 29

ACTIVITY 2.2
EXPRESSION MATCH

Provide students with sets of cards that have related Make Tens expressions. For example, one card might have 47 + 8 and a related card would have 50 + 5. Have students work together to pair cards. After students complete the activity, discuss how they knew the cards were related. During the discussion, focus not only on the fact that each card has the same sum but that some from one added are given to another to make a 10. Here are some examples of expressions you might use:

EXPRESSION	PAIRS WITH	PAIRS WITH
47 + 8	50 + 5	45 + 10
68 + 16	70 + 14	64 + 20
136 + 28	140 + 24	134 + 30

TEACHING TAKEAWAY

Expression cards can be made on index cards or something similar. Have a volunteer or students make them for you.

ACTIVITY 2.3
TWO-CARD EQUATIONS

Print and provide ten-frame cards to students. Have students select 2 ten-frame cards and record the expression. Then, have them rethink the expression using the Make Tens strategy and record the new Make Tens expression. Students should also record how they made the new equation. In the following example, the student says they gave 2 to 18 to make 20 + 4.

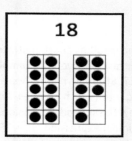
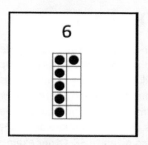

18 + 6
20 + 4

I gave 2 to 18

You can (and should) use cards with larger quantities to further develop and extend Make Tens. Keep in mind that for larger numbers you will need to give students a bit longer to absorb each quantity. Here is an example of what that might look like. Of course, you could easily pair 48 with the 6 or 18 above.

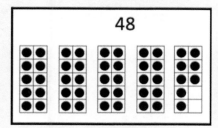
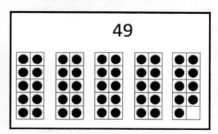

These ten-frame cards can be downloaded and used with this and other activities, including the "Paired Quick Looks" routine (Activity 2.6) later in this module.

(Continued)

(*Continued*)

RESOURCE(S) FOR THIS ACTIVITY

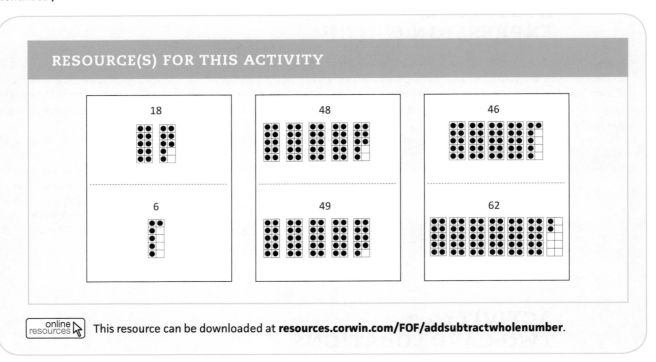

 This resource can be downloaded at **resources.corwin.com/FOF/addsubtractwholenumber**.

ACTIVITY 2.4
SAME AND DIFFERENT

It is important to understand how a strategy works and that the strategy yields the same result as another strategy. In this instructional activity, you pose two expressions and ask students to compare and contrast the two. For example, you could pose the question, "How is adding 35 + 38 like adding 33 + 40 and how is it different?" Students might then explain that they both yield the same sum of 73 but that the second expression is just adding a tens with no ones. Another group of students might say that they are the same because "you" just made a 10 to show the second expression. After working with 35 + 38 and 33 + 40, you could ask them to compare and contrast the original expression, 35 + 38, with 40 + 33 in which 5 is given to 35 instead of 2 being given to 38. Other examples for this task could be as follows:

33 + 38 and 31 + 40	67 + 17 and 70 + 14	59 + 47 and 60 + 46
134 + 56 and 140 + 50	28 + 155 and 30 + 153	77 + 231 and 78 + 230
251 + 287 and 250 + 288	918 + 125 and 920 + 123	612 + 446 and 608 + 450

ACTIVITY 2.5
PROMPTS FOR TEACHING MAKE TENS

Use the following prompts as opportunities to develop understanding of and reasoning with the strategy. Have students use representations and tools to justify their thinking, including base-10 models, number lines, number charts, and so on. After students work with the prompt(s), bring the class together to exchange ideas. These could be useful for collecting evidence of student understanding. Any prompt can be easily modified to feature different numbers (e.g., three-digit or four-digit numbers) and any prompt can be offered more than once if modified.

- Emi is working on 16 + 7. She thinks she can give some to 16 to make another 10. Do you agree? What would the new problem be? Does Emi's thinking always work? Show how you know if it does or doesn't.

- How can you make a 10 to solve 59 + 27? Create three new problems that you could also make a 10 to solve.

- Brian says that you can make a 10 for 395 + 405. Do you agree? What other problems could you solve by making a 10?

- You can make a 10 to solve 78 + 15 by thinking 78 + 2 + 13. Work with a partner to create new problems that can be solved in the same way.

- Manuel said that you can't use the Make Tens strategy for both 89 + 17 and 21 + 22. Which expression could Manuel be referring to? Why? Do you agree or disagree?

- To find the sum of 46 + 34, Daniel added 6 to both addends. Will this strategy work? Explain your thinking.

- Dylan wants to find the sum of 452 and 258. Show two different ways Dylan could solve this problem.

- Declan found two ways to rewrite this equation. He says they are different ways to get the same sum. Would you agree or disagree? Explain your thinking.

  519 + 634: 520 + 633 and 513 + 640

- How would you explain to a friend an efficient way to add 39 + 43?

- Explain how Shelly could use 124 + 250 to solve 126 + 248.

- Tell how the Make Tens strategy works. Create three expressions that you could use the Make Tens strategy to solve efficiently.

NOTES

_____

_____

_____

_____

_____

PRACTICE ACTIVITIES for Make Tens

Fluency is realized through quality practice that is focused, varied, processed, and connected. The activities in this section focus students' attention on how this strategy works and when to use it. The activities are a collection of varied engagements. The discussion you facilitate after an activity or the reflection prompts you attach to it should help students think about what they did mathematically, how they reasoned about the activity, and when the math they did (namely the strategy) might be useful. Debriefing should also help students see how the practice activity connects to recent instruction or how the strategy connects to other strategies they know. Game boards, recording sheets, digit cards, and other required materials are available as online resources for you to download, possibly modify, and use. As students work with activities, you want to look for how well they are acquiring the strategy and assimilating it into their collection of strategies.

FLUENCY COMPONENT	WHAT TO LOOK FOR AS STUDENTS PRACTICE THIS STRATEGY
Efficiency	• Are students using the Make Tens strategy efficiently? • Do they use the strategy regardless of its appropriateness for the problem at hand (e.g., 424 + 158 does not lend to Make Tens)?
Flexibility	• Are students using the Make Tens strategy when it is an appropriate option, or are they consistently counting on? • Are students carrying out the strategy in flexible ways? • Do they use the strategy for a variety of problems or only with a certain set of problems (e.g., only problems with two-digit addends, only problems with certain digits being used)? • Do they change their approach to or from this strategy as it proves inappropriate or overly complicated for the problem?
Accuracy	• Are students using the Make Tens strategy accurately? • Do they accurately make tens, hundreds, or thousands? • Are students finding accurate solutions? • Are they considering the reasonableness of their solutions?* • Are students estimating before finding solutions?*

*This consideration is not unique to this strategy and should be practiced throughout the pursuit of fluency with whole numbers.

WORKED EXAMPLES

Worked examples are problems that have been solved. Correctly worked examples can help students make sense of a strategy and incorrectly worked examples attend to common errors.

A true strength of the Make Tens strategy is that it is fairly error prone, building on students' understanding of place value. Here are two challenges that students commonly encounter:

1. The student has trouble determining the distance to a hundred or thousand.

   • 877 + 235: sees the 70 in 877 and thinks it is 33 away from 900 (not 23), so subtracts 33 from 235 to make 900.

   • 2,479 + 3,860: changes 3,860 to 3,900, not noticing they could change it to 4,000 (moving 140 over). The first option is less effective in making the problem easier to add.

2. The student makes the 10 or 100 but inaccurately adds/subtracts the change to the other number.

- 48 + 26: moves 2 from the 26 to the 48 to make 50, and rewrites the expression as 50 + 23.
- 507 + 366: takes 7 away from 507 to make 500, and rewrites/thinks 500 + 372.

The instructional prompts from Activity 2.5 can be used for collecting examples. Throughout the module are various worked examples that you can use as fictional worked examples. A sampling of additional ideas is provided in the following table.

SAMPLE WORKED EXAMPLES FOR MAKE TENS

Correctly Worked Example (make sense of the strategy) What did _____ do? Why does it work? Is this a good method for this problem?	Shanice's work: $\begin{array}{r} 68 \\ +36 \\ \hline \end{array}$ $\begin{array}{r} 70 \\ +34 \\ \hline 104 \end{array}$
Partially Worked Example (implement the strategy accurately) Why did _____ start the problem this way? What does _____ need to do to finish the problem?	Brandon's start: $\begin{array}{l} 4{,}375 + 2{,}840 \\ -160 \qquad\ \downarrow \\ \qquad\quad 3{,}000 \end{array}$
Incorrectly Worked Example (highlight common errors) What did _____ do? What mistake does _____ make? How can this mistake be fixed?	James's work: $592 + 475 =$ $600 + 468 = 1{,}068$

ACTIVITY 2.6

Name: "Paired Quick Looks"   **Type:** Routine

About the Routine: Ten-frame cards and other representations help students see how a 10 is made. This routine offers a quick look at two numbers and students have to think about how they can make tens to combine the numbers efficiently.

Materials: Quick Look ten-frame cards

Directions: 1. Show two cards for students to look at quickly.

2. Have students determine how many there are altogether.

3. Partners discuss how they put the quantities together to find the total.

4. Students then share their thinking with the whole group.

5. As students share, you record the equation(s) that go with it.

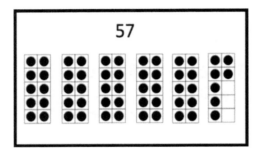 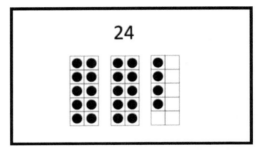

For this example, you show the 57 and 24 cards quickly. Students talk about the sum and how they found it. During the whole group discussion, you record 57 + 24 and the new expression that students thought about, such as 60 + 21, and then record the sum they found.

RESOURCE(S) FOR THIS ACTIVITY

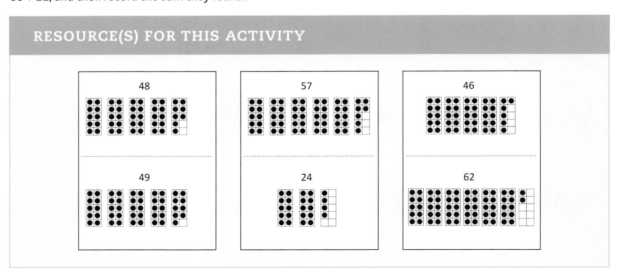

online resources ⌐ This resource can be downloaded at **resources.corwin.com/FOF/addsubtractwholenumber**.

ACTIVITY 2.7

Name: "Say It As a Make Tens"   **Tupe:** Routine

About the Routine: This routine explicitly charges students with renaming expressions as an equivalent expression after making 10. The routine would also work well with other strategies.

Materials: Prepare expressions for students to rename.

Directions: In this routine, you pose two or three expressions to students and they discuss another way to say it (SanGiovanni, 2019). While there are many ways an expression can be restated, you want to focus their attention to restating it by using the Make Tens strategy. In a third-grade class, you might pose these expressions:

Say It As a Make Tens		
138 + 56	219 + 64	71 + 489

Students would discuss with partners how to use 10 to rename the expression. The first could be thought of as 140 + 54 or 134 + 60. After partners talk, the whole group shares their thinking. Be sure to record their new expressions just below the original. Keep in mind that you can adjust the routine as needed. For example, you might have students work one expression at a time rather than all of the expressions you post at once. In time, the routine can be adjusted to extend to Make Hundreds or Make Thousands.

Say It As Make Hundreds		
479 + 690	792 + 348	525 + 885

Say It As Make Thousands		
4295 + 1690	3925 + 1475	5450 + 6985

ACTIVITY 2.8

Name: "This is Like _____ Because" **Type:** Routine

About the Routine: Basic facts with +8 and +9 can be recalled with a Making 10 or Pretend-a-10 (Compensation) strategy. This routine helps students connect and extend their basic fact understanding.

Materials: Prepare a collection of related expressions in one row as shown.

Directions: Prompt students with a basic fact and three or four related expressions. In small groups, students turn-and-talk to describe how the basic fact is similar to the expression. Then, the whole group comes back together to share their thinking. The examples in the following figure show the range and flexibility of the routine. In the first row, 9 + 7 is a basic fact. Each of the following examples uses a 10 as well even though they don't feature the same number of ones in each addend. The second row includes a Combination of 10 fact and the following expressions use that strategy in some capacity. The remaining rows provide more examples of extending a basic fact to similar problems with a larger addend. The second table repeats this idea of building from a basic fact, with a focus on subtraction. In each case, students complete the sentence frame—for example, saying "23 – 9 is like 13 – 9 because . . .

- 23 also ends in a 3.

- 23 is just 10 more than 13.

- both can be solved by subtracting 10 and adding 1.

THIS	THIS IS LIKE ___ BECAUSE		
	IS LIKE ___ BECAUSE	IS LIKE ___ BECAUSE	IS LIKE ___ BECAUSE
9 + 7	19 + 5	29 + 8	329 + 6
6 + 4	16 + 4	260 + 40	356 + 4
8 + 5	18 + 5	38 + 5	258 + 5
7 + 6	17 + 6	170 + 60	370 + 460

THIS	THIS IS LIKE ___ BECAUSE		
	IS LIKE ___ BECAUSE	IS LIKE ___ BECAUSE	IS LIKE ___ BECAUSE
13 – 9	23 – 9	53 – 9	413 – 9
10 – 7	20 – 7	60 – 7	330 – 7
15 – 8	25 – 8	35 – 8	565 – 8
12 – 9	22 – 9	52 – 9	472 – 9

ACTIVITY 2.9

Name: Make It, Take It   **Type:** Game

About the Game: *Make It, Take It* engages students in practicing making the same 10 in a variety of ways. It extends students' understanding of the basic fact strategy that makes a 10. The goal of the game is to be the first player to take away all 10 counters.

Materials: *Make It, Take It* game board, 10 chips or markers, 10-sided die for each student

Directions:
1. Players place their 10 chips on their game board at random. They can place more than one chip on any space.

2. Players then take turns rolling a digit to make the targeted 10 (40 in the example).

3. They take a chip from the number if it combines with the number rolled to make the targeted 10.

4. The first player who removes all of their chips wins the game.

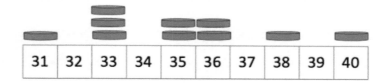

In this example, players are playing *Make It, Take It* to make 40. The player has put 10 counters on the game board. On this player's first turn, she rolled a 5. She could remove one chip from 35 because 35 and 5 make 40. But note that she doesn't remove both chips on 35. On her second turn, she rolled an 8 and loses her turn because she has no game piece on 32. The game continues until she removes all of her chips.

RESOURCE(S) FOR THIS ACTIVITY

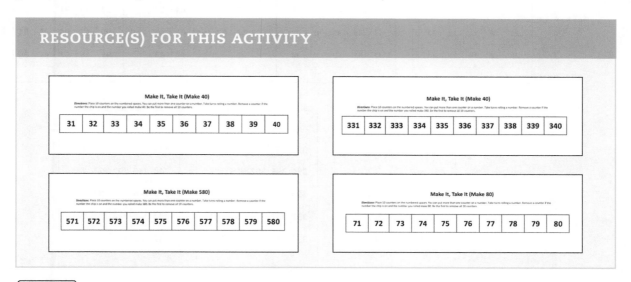

online resources ➤ This resource can be downloaded at **resources.corwin.com/FOF/addsubtractwholenumber**.

ACTIVITY 2.10

Name: A Winning Streak   **Type:** Game

About the Game: *Winning Streak* practices adding a one-digit number to the same "close-to-10" addend. It can be modified to practice the concept with a variety of addends as shown.

Materials: *Winning Streak* game board per pair, 10-sided die or digit cards (0–9) or deck of cards (with kings and jacks removed; queens = 0 and aces = 1); two-colored counters

Directions:
1. Each player takes turns rolling a number and adding it to 19. If a player rolls (draws) a 0 (queen), 1 (ace), or 2, they lose their turn.

2. Players then place a counter on the sum. For example, if player 1 rolls an 8, they add that to 19 and can then choose any available 27 and place one of player 1's counters.

3. A player tries to get three, four, or five spaces in a row. Getting three in a row earns 5 points, four in a row earns 10 points, and five in a row earns 20 points. Rows can overlap, but only by one square.

4. The game ends when the spaces are filled.

5. The players then add up their points and the player with the highest score wins.

RESOURCE(S) FOR THIS ACTIVITY

A Winning Streak (+19)

22	24	26	27	23
25	27	23	27	26
24	26	22	25	25
23	28	25	28	22
22	26	28	23	24

A Winning Streak (+39)

42	44	46	47	43
45	47	43	47	46
44	46	42	45	45
43	48	45	48	42
42	46	48	43	44

A Winning Streak (+58)

61	63	65	66	62
64	66	62	65	65
63	64	61	64	63
62	67	64	67	61
61	65	67	62	63

A Winning Streak (+87)

91	93	95	96	92
94	96	92	95	95
93	90	91	94	93
92	96	94	92	91
91	95	97	92	90

A Winning Streak (+459)

462	464	466	467	463
465	467	463	467	466
464	466	462	465	465
463	468	465	468	462
462	466	468	463	464

A Winning Streak (+388)

391	393	395	396	392
394	396	392	395	395
393	394	391	394	393
392	397	394	397	391
391	395	397	392	393

A Winning Streak (+237)

241	243	245	246	242
244	246	242	245	245
243	240	241	244	243
242	247	244	246	241
241	245	246	242	240

online resources These resources can be downloaded at **resources.corwin.com/FOF/addsubtractwholenumber**.

ACTIVITY 2.11

Name: *Give Some to Make Ten*   **Type:** *Game*

About the Game: *Give Some to Make Ten* focuses students' attention on an amount they would give from one addend to another to make a 10 or 100. It helps students focus on what is "broken apart" and moved from one number to the other.

Materials: one *Give Some to Make Ten* game board and one regular six-sided die per pair of students

Directions:

1. Players take turns rolling the die to generate a number.

2. The player uses that number to look for an expression in which the amount rolled could be given from one addend to the other to make use of the Make Tens strategy.

3. For example, a player rolls a 4. She chooses the expression 76 + 24 because she could give 4 from 24 to 76 to make 80 + 20. Or, she could have put her chip on the space for 86 + 27 because she could give 4 from 27 to 86 to make 90 + 23.

4. If a player rolls a number that can't be used with any of the remaining expressions, that player loses their turn.

5. The game ends when all of the spaces are filled.

6. The player who has the most three-in-a-rows wins the game.

RESOURCE(S) FOR THIS ACTIVITY

Give Some to Make Ten

Directions: Take turns rolling a number. Choose a space on the game board where the amount you roll could be given from one addend to the other to show the Make Tens strategy. The game ends when all spaces are covered. The player with the most three-in-a-rows wins.

99 + 98	38 + 12	39 + 16	76 + 24	16 + 77
37 + 69	17 + 25	38 + 63	48 + 23	89 + 26
97 + 5	88 + 17	47 + 54	86 + 27	25 + 38
68 + 33	59 + 13	68 + 29	77 + 17	99 + 58
27 + 44	57 + 43	68 + 27	46 + 27	35 + 46

This resource can be downloaded at **resources.corwin.com/FOF/addsubtractwholenumber**.

ACTIVITY 2.12

Name: Making Make Tens (or Hundreds)   **Type:** Center

About the Center: This center focuses students' attention on writing equivalent expressions by changing an original expression into one that has a tens or hundreds addend. It can be used to complement Activity 2.7 ("Say It As a Make Tens").

Materials: digit cards (1–9) or playing cards (ace = 1, 10s and face cards removed), Making Make Tens (or Hundreds) recording sheet

Directions: 1. Students use digit cards to make two addends.

2. Students record the expression.

3. Students think about how they could solve the problem using the Make Tens strategy.

4. Students write the new expression and find the sum.

For example, a student working with two-digit addends pulls four digit cards to make her two addends. She pulls 9, 4, 3, and 5. She arranges them to make 35 + 49. She rethinks the problem as 34 + 50 and records the sum as 84. Then, she reshuffles the digit cards and creates a new problem.

TEACHING TAKEAWAY

You can modify any activity. Here, direct students to pull five digit cards to make a three-digit and a two-digit addend for this center.

RESOURCE(S) FOR THIS ACTIVITY

Making Make Tens

Directions: Use four digit cards to make two addends. Record the problem. Rethink the problem using the Make Tens strategy and then record the problem.

My Problem	My New Make Tens Problem	Sum
35 + 49	34 + 50	84

Making Make Hundreds

Directions: Use six digit cards to make two addends. Record the problem. Rethink the problem using the Make Tens strategy and then record the problem.

My Problem	My New Make Tens Problem	Sum
275 + 386	300 + 361	661

online resources These resources can be downloaded at **resources.corwin.com/FOF/addsubtractwholenumber**.

ACTIVITY 2.13

Name: Combinations Solitaire   **Type:** Center

About the Center: This is a single-player card game for students to practice finding combinations that equal 10, a multiple of 10, or 100.

VERSION 1: MAKING 10

Materials: four sets of digit cards or a deck of playing cards with tens and face cards removed

Directions: 1. The player deals themselves five cards face up in front of them.

2. The player then deals three more "pairing cards" above their row of cards. The goal is to use the player's five cards to make a 10 with the pairing cards. Here is an example:

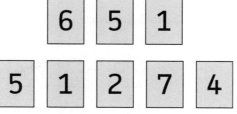

In this example, the 5 matches with the 5 to make a combination and remove it. The 6 combines with 4 to make a 10 and it can be removed. The 1, 2, and 7 can't be used.

3. Next, the player replaces all three pairing cards to try to remove the remaining cards. Here is another example:

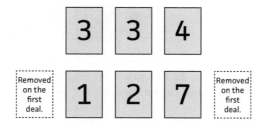

In this example, a 3 and 7 make a 10 to remove one more of the original five cards. There are no other matches and a new set of three cards is dealt. The activity continues until the original five cards are removed.

VERSION 2: MAKE TENS

Materials: deck of two-digit number cards (e.g., 10, 11 … 99) and deck of digit cards (0–9)

Directions: 1. A player deals 5 two-digit cards face up as shown below.

$$\boxed{35}\ \boxed{31}\ \boxed{32}\ \boxed{37}\ \boxed{34}$$

(Continued)

(*Continued*)

2. The player deals 3 one-digit cards to pair with their two-digit cards to make tens. For example, the 8 could be used with 32 to make a 10 (40) and the 32 card would be removed.

| 4 | 8 | 3 |

| 35 | 31 | 32 | 37 | 34 |

3. The goal is to remove all of the two-digit cards.

VERSION 3: MAKE ONE HUNDRED

Materials: deck of two-digit number cards (e.g., 10, 11 … 99) and deck of digit cards **(0–9)**

Directions: 1. A player deals 5 two-digit cards.

| 75 | 21 | 42 | 27 | 11 |

2. The player deals four digit cards above the two-digit cards.

| 6 | 3 | 4 | 7 |

| 75 | 21 | 42 | 27 | 11 |

3. The player pairs two of the digit cards to make a two-digit number that matches one of the two-digit cards to make a hundred. For example, a 7 and a 3 could form 73 or 37. The 73 is a match to the 27 card, so 27 can be removed.

4. The goal is to remove the 5 two-digit cards dealt.

RESOURCE(S) FOR THIS ACTIVITY

1	2	3	4
5	6	7	8
9	10	11	12
13	14	15	16
17	18	19	20

41	42	43	44
45	46	47	48
49	50	51	52
53	54	55	56
57	58	59	60

81	82	83	84
85	86	87	88
89	90	91	92
93	94	95	96
97	98	99	

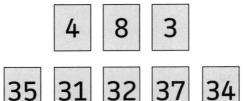

online resources ☞ This resource can be downloaded at **resources.corwin.com/FOF/addsubtractwholenumber**.

ACTIVITY 2.14

Name: Rewrite It   **Type:** Center

About the Center: This center is designed for students to practice rewriting expressions to use the Make Tens, Make Hundreds, or Make Thousands strategy.

Materials: Rewrite It center cards and recording sheet

Directions:
1. Students select a card at random and record it on their recording sheet. Students rethink the expression by making a 10 and record the new expression.

2. Then, students record the sum using their math journals or with the recording sheet.

Examples of problems for expression cards to use with this center include the following:

TEACHING TAKEAWAY

Recording sheets help students progress through an activity, organize their thinking, and show accountability.

RESOURCE(S) FOR THIS ACTIVITY

Rewrite It

Directions: Pull a problem card. Think about how you can use 10 to rethink the problem. Write the new problem. Write the sum. Try again.

Problem	Rethinking the Problem by Making Ten	Sum

19 + 18	33 + 48
27 + 19	43 + 27
37 + 46	61 + 29
99 + 63	59 + 12
94 + 77	26 + 85

265 + 118	779 + 121
461 + 329	597 + 454
628 + 143	234 + 649
297 + 165	119 + 935
278 + 593	852 + 429

1,069 + 2,093	7,647 + 7,636
3,117 + 3,229	4,121 + 4,269
4,119 + 1,452	6,543 + 5,638
2,523 + 2,547	9,019 + 1,018
9,601 + 9,102	1,029 + 1,601

online resources ⌐ Center cards and this recording sheet can be downloaded at **resources.corwin.com/FOF/ addsubtractwholenumber**.

ACTIVITY 2.15

Name: Changing Addends, Changing Sums   **Type:** Center

About the Center: Changing addends influences the sum. For example, adding 10 more will yield a sum that is 10 more. This center has students create an addend and add it to related addends and observe how the sum changes from the previous problem.

Materials: digit cards (0–9) or playing cards (queens = 0, aces = 1, kings and jacks removed); Changing Addends, Changing Sums recording sheet

Directions:
1. Students turn over two digit cards and create a two-digit number to add to the numbers provided in the center.

2. Students find the sum of their number and the "Added to" number.

3. After finding each new sum, students tell how the new sum relates to the previous sum.

This center can offer countless practice opportunities. The top example shows how to change addends by one, while the bottom shows how to change addends by hundreds.

> **TEACHING TAKEAWAY**
>
> Centers are good opportunities for practice. To maximize center effectiveness, take time to teach a center so that students understand how it works.

ADDENDS THAT CHANGE BY ONE

My Number	Added to	Sum (show how you found the sum)	How is this sum related to the sum above?
	99		
	98		
	97		

ADDENDS THAT CHANGE BY HUNDREDS

My Number	Added to	Sum (show how you found the sum)	How is this sum related to the sum above?
	97		
	197		

 Digit cards and this recording sheet can be downloaded at **resources.corwin.com/FOF/ addsubtractwholenumber**.

NOTES

Partial Sums and Differences Strategy

STRATEGY OVERVIEW:
Partial Sums and Differences

What is Partial Sums and Differences? This strategy refers to the process of adding or subtracting place values, starting with the largest place value and moving to the smallest (the reverse of standard algorithms). When no regrouping is involved, the Partials strategy is straightforward—just add or subtract each place value. In other cases, the regrouping is captured when recomposing the parts.

HOW DO PARTIAL SUMS AND DIFFERENCES WORK?

This is a break apart strategy that involves decomposing, often by place value, to compute and then puts the partial sums back together. It should be a *flexible* process wherein students decide if they want to decompose both addends or just one. Recording can be vertical or horizontal. Here are a few examples:

PROBLEM: 37 + 38	PROBLEM: 477 + 1,258
Horizontal	Horizontal
37 + 38	477 + 1,258
30 + 30 = 60 7 + 8 = 15	400 + 1,200 = 1,600 70 + 50 = 120 7 + 8 = 15
60 + 15 = 75	1,600 + 120 + 15 = 1,735
Vertical	Vertical
37 + 38 60 + 15 75	1,258 + 477 1,600 120 + 15 1,735

PROBLEM: 242 + 658	PROBLEM: 1,407 + 8,755
Horizontal	By Place Value
242 + 658	1,407 + 8,755
200 + 600 = 800 42 + 58 = 100	1,000 + 8,000 = 9,000 406 + 700 = 1,100 7 + 55 = 62 10,162
800 + 100 = 900	
Partial Sums and Make Thousands	
1,407 + 8,755	
1,300 + 8,700 = 10,000 107 + 55 = 162 10,162	

When no regrouping is required, Partial Differences can be done in writing or mentally.

PROBLEM: 47 – 34	PROBLEM: 658 – 242	PROBLEM: 8,755 – 1,203
Horizontal	Horizontal	Horizontal
$47 - 34$	$658 - 242$	$8,755 - 1,203$
$40 - 30 = 10$ $7 - 4 = 3$ $10 + 3 = 13$	$600 - 200 = 400$ $50 - 40 = 10$ $8 - 2 = 6$ $400 + 10 + 6 = 416$	$8,000 - 1,000 = 7,000$ $700 - 200 = 500$ $50 - 0 = 50$ $5 - 3 = 2$ $7,000 + 500 + 50 + 2 = 7,552$
Vertical	Vertical	Vertical
$\begin{array}{r} 47 \\ -\ 34 \\ \hline 10 \\ +\ \ 3 \\ \hline 13 \end{array}$	$\begin{array}{r} 658 \\ -\ 242 \\ \hline 400 \\ 10 \\ +\ \ 6 \\ \hline 416 \end{array}$	$\begin{array}{r} 8,755 \\ -\ 1,203 \\ \hline 7,000 \\ 500 \\ 50 \\ +\ \ 2 \\ \hline 7,552 \end{array}$

When regrouping is required, Partial Differences will involve negative numbers, which have not been introduced. The following table offers two ways to explain Partial Differences, one using integer language (left) and the other using the zero properties with no reference to negative numbers (right).

USING INTEGER LANGUAGE	USING ALTERNATIVE LANGUAGE AND NOTATION
$\begin{array}{r} 524 \\ -\ 137 \\ \hline 400 \\ -10 \\ +\ -3 \\ \hline 387 \end{array}$ subtract hundreds 400 subtract tens (−10) subtract ones (−3) ← combine	Subtract hundreds: 400 Subtract tens: 20 – 30 Break apart: 20 – 20 – 10 [**still need to** subtract 10] Subtract ones: 4 – 7 Break apart: 4 – 4 – 3 [**still need to** subtract 3] Combine: 400 – 10 – 3 = **387**

WHEN DO YOU CHOOSE PARTIAL SUMS AND DIFFERENCES?

When no regrouping is needed, this strategy is what we do. Unlike some other strategies wherein the numbers "lend" themselves to the strategy, this strategy is almost always applicable (like the standard algorithm) but perhaps not most efficient (e.g., 998 + 1,345 is more efficiently solved with Make a Thousand than Partial Sums). Partials are an effective replacement for standard algorithms (the front-end left-to-right approach and lack of "tick mark" notations make it more accessible).

MODULE 1 Count On/ Count Back

MODULE 2 Make Tens Strategy

MODULE 3 Partial Sums and Differences Strategy

MODULE 4 Compensation Strategy

MODULE 5 Think Addition Strategy

MODULE 6 Standard Algorithms for Addition and Subtraction

PARTIAL SUMS AND DIFFERENCES:
Strategy Briefs for Families

It is important that families understand the strategies and know how they work so that they can be partners in the pursuit of fluency. These strategy briefs are a tool for doing that. You can include them in parent or school newsletters or share them at parent conferences. They are available for download so that you can adjust them as needed.

Partial Sums Strategy

How It Works: We can break apart addends in different ways. We add the parts to find partial sums. Then, we can add the partial sums together to find the answer.

1.   Choose how to break apart the addends.
2.   Add the parts to find each partial sum.
3.   Add the partial sums.

The left example shows that 477 + 258 can be broken apart by place value. Add the hundreds together, add the tens together, then add the ones together. Then, each of those partial sums is added to find the answer to the original problem.

The right example isn't broken apart by place value because the person noticed that 42 and 58 make a hundred and broke apart the addends differently.

When It's Useful: This strategy is useful unless another strategy can be applied more efficiently.

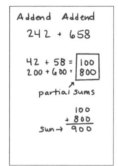

Partial Differences Strategy

How It Works: We can break apart addends in different ways. We can subtract the parts to find partial differences. Then, we can add the partial differences together to find the answer.

1.   Choose how to break apart the numbers.
2.   Subtract the parts to find each partial difference.
3.   Add the partial differences.

The left example shows that 547 − 236 can be broken apart by place value. Subtract the hundreds, subtract the tens, then subtract the ones. Then, each of those partial differences is added to find the answer to the original problem.

The right example shows that the partial difference is a negative number. When you subtract the hundreds, 500 − 400 is 100. But when you subtract the tens and ones, it gives you negative numbers: 20 − 30 is − 10 and 4 − 7 is − 3. You will take those amounts away at the end. So, 10 and then 3 is then subtracted from 400.

When It's Useful: This strategy is useful but sometimes not used because of the possibility that you'll have to use negative numbers.

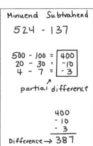

 These resources can be downloaded at **resources.corwin.com/FOF/addsubtractwholenumber**.

NOTES

_____

_____

_____

TEACHING ACTIVITIES for Partial Sums and Differences

Before students are able to choose strategies, which is a key to fluency, they first must be able to understand and use relevant strategies. These activities focus on the strategy of Partial Sums and Differences. While students may employ other methods, which is appropriate, they must understand how this strategy works, be able to implement it mentally, and become familiar with examples of problems in which they will want to use it.

ACTIVITY 3.1
BAG OF BLOCKS

Bag of Blocks is an activity for adding or subtracting partials using base-10 blocks. It can be completed as a partner activity or through a set of rotations. The activity can be easily recycled as an independent learning center as well.

First, put base-10 blocks in small paper bags. Label the bags with letters. Students empty each bag and record the amount. Then, students find the total amount of blocks in both bags by using the Partial Sums strategy. Students record their thinking in their math journals or on the recording sheet provided. This activity can be modified easily to add two-digit, three-digit, or four-digit addends and you can choose to use a different tool, like place value disks, instead of base-10 blocks.

RESOURCE(S) FOR THIS ACTIVITY

Bag of Blocks

Directions: Empty both bags of blocks. Record the number in each bag. Find the sum of the blocks using the Partial Sums strategy.

Bag	Bag	Sum (showing partial sums)
359	122	300 + 300 = 900 50 + 20 = 70 9 + 2 = 6 900 + 70 + 6 = 976

ACTIVITY 3.2
PARTIAL SUMS WITH EXPANDER CARDS

Expander cards are foldables that allow students to see a number through place value. The lead place value is shown on top and the trailing zeros can be folded back accordion style as a way to "tuck" them behind the top digit. Expander cards can be downloaded on the companion site.

RESOURCE(S) FOR THIS ACTIVITY

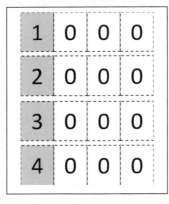

 Expander cards can be downloaded at **resources.corwin.com/FOF/addsubtractwholenumber**.

For this activity, give students an expression to complete, such as 123 + 456. Students represent the expression with a set of expander cards folded so that the zeros are not showing.

$$123 + 456 =$$

Then students unfold the cards to show the value of each digit and find each pair partial sums.

$$123 + 456 =$$
$$100 + 400 =$$
$$20 + 50 =$$
$$3 + 6 =$$

TEACHING TAKEAWAY
Once understanding of this strategy is established, expander cards can become a good center activity.

Students should record both the original expression and the set of expanded expressions. Discuss with students how the two sets are similar and different. Connect this work to base-10 models or number lines as needed. This instructional activity can also make a good center after students show understanding of the strategy.

ACTIVITY 3.3
MAKING CONNECTIONS

Solid conceptual understanding of any strategy is evidenced through a variety of representations and connections between them. In this activity, students are shown how to use partial sums with three different representations, including base-10 blocks, number lines, and numerical expressions (Partial Sums, lower left in the following image). Students are also asked if Partial Sums is the best way to solve the expression. There are a few things to keep in mind about this activity. First, it should be used to confirm understanding of the strategy. Once confirmed, you do not want students to continue to show Partial Sums or any other strategy in a variety of ways but instead simply as symbols (equations). Also note that Part 3 goes into greater detail about strategy selection. Even so, when developing any strategy, it is important to have students consider if the strategy is useful for the problem at hand. You can choose to include it as shown in the image or pose other prompts such as "Create a new problem to solve with Partial Sums" or "Show another way to solve the problem." You can also modify the graphic organizer to have only three sections.

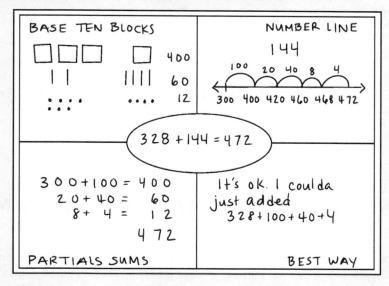

 This resource can be downloaded at **resources.corwin.com/FOF/addsubtractwholenumber**.

ACTIVITY 3.4
THE MISSING PROBLEM

This problem-based activity is an opportunity to extend or enrich instruction with Partial Sums and Differences. You pose a set of equations with unknowns that represent the partial sums and then students find the unknowns and put the equations back together to determine the original problem.

> In a Partial Sums example of "The Missing Problem," you pose
>
> $80 + \underline{\hspace{0.5cm}} = 170$ $9 + \underline{\hspace{0.5cm}} = 13$
>
> Students find the unknowns 90 and 4.
>
> They determine that the original problem was 89 + 94 and validate their thinking by showing the original problem with partial sums.

(Continued)

(Continued)

In a Partial Sums example of "The Missing Problem," you pose

700 + _____ = 1,000   40 + _____ = 60   7 + _____ = 11

Students find the unknowns to be 300, 20, and 4.

They determine that the original problem was 747 + 324 and validate their thinking by showing the original problem with partial sums.

In a Partial Differences example of "The Missing Problem," you pose

300 – _____ = 100   20 – _____ = 10   4 – _____ = 2

Students find the unknowns to be 200, 10, and 2.

They determine that the original problem was 324 – 212 and validate their thinking by showing the original problem with partial differences.

In a Partial Differences example of "The Missing Problem," you pose

1,000 – _____ = 1,000   300 – _____ = –100   70 – _____ = 40   2 – _____ = –7

Students find the unknowns to be 0, 400, 30, and 9.

They determine the original problem to be 1,372 – 439 and validate their thinking by showing the original problem with partial differences.

ACTIVITY 3.5
PROMPTS FOR TEACHING PARTIAL SUMS AND DIFFERENCES

Use the following prompts as opportunities to develop understanding of and reasoning with the strategy. Have students use representations and tools to justify their thinking, including base-10 models, number lines, number charts, and so on. After students work with the prompt(s), bring the class together to exchange ideas. These could be useful for collecting evidence of student understanding. Any prompt can be easily modified to feature different numbers (e.g., three-digit or four-digit numbers) and any prompt can be offered more than once if modified.

- Juan solved 36 + 57. His work is below. Tell why you agree or disagree with Juan.

$$30 + 50 = 80$$
$$6 + 7 = 13$$
$$80 + 13 = 93$$

- The class was working on solving 82 – 25. Jameel solved the problem like this:

$$82 - 25$$

70   12   20   5

$$70 - 20 = 50$$
$$12 - 5 = 7$$
$$50 + 7 = 57$$

Do you agree with Jameel? Explain your thinking.

- Daniel solved a problem using the Partial Sums strategy seen here. Tell how you know what might have been the original expression.

$$400 + 600 = 1,000$$
$$20 + 30 = 50$$
$$8 + 7 = 15$$

$$1,000 + 50 + 15 = 1,065$$

- Tell how the Partial Sums strategy works. Create three expressions that you can solve efficiently with partial sums.

- Dee used the Partial Differences strategy to solve 342 – 170. See her work shown here. What does she have to do next? Why does she have –30 as part of her work?

$$342 - 170$$

$$300 - 100 = 200$$
$$40 - 70 = -30$$
$$2 - 0 = 2$$

- Kai used partial differences to subtract 516 – 274. Tell if you agree or disagree with Kai's work. Explain your thinking.

$$516 - 274 = 362$$

$$500 - 200 = 300$$
$$70 - 10 = 60$$
$$6 - 4 = 2$$
$$\overline{ 362}$$

- The difference of 2 four-digit numbers is 475. What might those numbers be? Use Partial Differences to show you know the difference of the numbers is 475.

- Two different numbers don't have a zero in them. When added, the sum is between 1,500 and 1,750. Use Partial Sums to show what those numbers might be.

- Create two different problems that wouldn't be good for solving with the Partial Sums strategy. Tell why these problems aren't good for the Partial Sums strategy.

- Timothy used partial sums to solve the problem shown here. Juan said there is an error in Timothy's work. Can you find the mistake that Timothy made?

```
  7 4 1
+   2 9
  9 0 0
    6 0
    1 0
  9 7 0
```

- Francesca used partial differences to solve the problem shown here. Juan said there is an error in her work. Who is correct? How do you know?

```
  7 4 9
-   2 1
  5 0 0
    2 0
      8
  5 2 8
```

PRACTICE ACTIVITIES for Partial Sums and Differences

Fluency is realized through quality practice that is focused, varied, processed, and connected. The activities in this section focus students' attention on how this strategy works and when to use it. The activities are a collection of varied engagements. The discussion you facilitate after an activity or the reflection prompts you attach to it should help students think about what they did mathematically, how they reasoned about the activity, and when the math they did (namely the strategy) might be useful. Debriefing should also help students see how the practice activity connects to recent instruction or how the strategy connects to other strategies they know. Game boards, recording sheets, digit cards, and other required materials are available as online resources for you to download, possibly modify, and use. As students work with activities, you want to look for how well they are acquiring the strategy and assimilating it into their collection of strategies.

FLUENCY COMPONENT	WHAT TO LOOK FOR AS STUDENTS PRACTICE THIS STRATEGY
Efficiency	• Are students using Partial Sums and Differences or are they reverting to previously learned and/or possibly less appropriate strategies? • Are students using the Partial Sums and Differences strategy efficiently? • Do they use the strategy regardless of its appropriateness for the problem at hand?
Flexibility	• Are students avoiding the Partial Sums and Differences strategy or using it solely? • Are students breaking apart numbers in a variety of ways? Do they always decompose by place value? • Are students decomposing both numbers consistently or are they choosing which number to decompose? • Are students carrying out the strategy in flexible ways? (e.g., sometimes decomposing by place value, sometimes using friendly numbers, sometimes decomposing just one number) • Do they change their approach to or from the strategy as it proves inappropriate or overly complicated for the problem?
Accuracy	• Are students using the Partial Sums and Differences strategy accurately? • Are students finding accurate solutions? • Are they considering the reasonableness of their solutions?* • Are students estimating before finding solutions?*

*This consideration is not unique to this strategy and should be practiced throughout the pursuit of fluency with whole numbers.

WORKED EXAMPLES

Worked examples are problems that have been solved. Correctly worked examples can help students make sense of a strategy and incorrectly worked examples attend to common errors.

As you have read, Partial Sums and Differences can become rote. Worked examples can help introduce other ways to make use of this strategy. Incorrectly worked examples can highlight common challenges or errors when using the Partial Sums and Differences strategy:

1. The student subtracts when the subtrahend place value is larger than the digit in the minuend.

   - 528 – 255: subtracts 20 – 50 and gets 30 as a partial difference.

2. The student makes adding errors when adding the partials together.

   - 237 + 546: adds 200 + 500 to equal 700, 30 + 70 to equal 100, and 7 + 6 to equal 13, but records the answer as 723.

The instructional prompts from Activity 3.5 provide numerous worked examples. Throughout the module are more worked examples that you can use. A sampling of additional ideas is provided in the following table.

SAMPLE WORKED EXAMPLES FOR PARTIAL SUMS AND DIFFERENCES

	ADDITION	SUBTRACTION
Correctly Worked Example (make sense of the strategy) What did _____ do? Why does it work? Is this a good method for this problem?	Manuel's work for 5,755 + 1,389: $5,700 + 1,300 = 7,000$ $50 + 80 = 130$ $5 + 9 = 14$ $\overline{7,144}$	Aaliyah's work for 925 – 548: $900 - 500 = 400$ $20 - 20 - 20 = \text{subtract } 20$ $5 - 5 - 3 = \text{subtract } 3$ $400 - 20 - 3 = 377$
Partially Worked Example (implement the strategy accurately) Why did _____ start the problem this way? What does _____ need to do to finish the problem?	Cari's start for 767 + 289: $750 + 250 = 1,000$	Lorilee's start for 3,480 – 1,839: $3,400 - 1,400 = 2,000$
Incorrectly Worked Example (highlight common errors) What did _____ do? What mistake does _____ make? How can this mistake be fixed?	Tamika's work for 44,206 + 6,347: $4,400 + 600 = 500$ $200 + 300 = 500$ $47 + 6 = 53$ $\overline{1,053}$	Aiko's work for 319 – 156: $200 + 40 + 3 = 243$

ACTIVITY 3.6

Name: "The Parts"　　　　　　　　　　**Type:** Routine

About the Routine: "The Parts" is a routine for reasoning and reinforcing Partial Sums and Differences. Any problem can be solved with partial sums and differences. And, as you know, many problems will have similar partials. This routine helps students see that different problems can have the same partial sum of 900, 70, or 14. It also aims to develop critical thinking and reasoning.

Materials: prepared Partial Sums equation, whiteboards or sticky notes for students (optional)

Directions:　1. Give clues for students to interpret.

　　　　　　　2. Students use the clues to create partials of an addition or subtraction problem.

　　　　　　　3. Students compare their thinking with a partner before finding out whether anyone in the class has created a problem that matches the teacher's problem.

"The Parts": Partial Sums Example

Teacher writes on the board: 900

Teacher poses: The sum of the hundreds is 900. What might the hundreds of each addend be?

Students determine a possibility and share their thinking. For example, Oscar thinks 300 + 600.

Teacher writes on the board: 70

Teacher poses: The sum of the tens is 70. What might the tens of each addend be?

Students determine a possibility and share their thinking. For example, Oscar thinks 20 + 50.

Teacher writes on the board: 14

Teacher poses: The sum of the ones is 14. What might the ones of each addend be?

Students determine a possibility and share their thinking. For example, Oscar thinks 7 + 7.

Teacher poses: What are the two addends you came up with?

Oscar records 327 + 657 and shares his expression with a partner.

The teacher solicits different expressions reinforcing that each has the sum of 984. The teacher reveals her Partial Sums problem and celebrates with the class if anyone has created the same problem. In this example, the teacher's problem was 423 + 561. The teacher might then have students compare and contrast their expression with the teacher's, noting how certain place values are similar.

"The Parts": Partial Differences Example

Teacher writes on the board: 400

Teacher poses: The difference of the hundreds is 400. What might the hundreds of each addend be?

Students determine a possibility and share their thinking. For example, Kristen thinks 600 – 200.

Teacher writes on the board: –50

Teacher poses: The difference of the tens is –50. What might the tens of each addend be?

Students determine a possibility and share their thinking. For example, Kristen thinks 20 – 70.

Teacher writes on the board: 3

Teacher poses: The difference of the ones is 3. What might the ones of each addend be?

Students determine a possibility and share their thinking. For example, Kristen thinks 5 – 2.

Teacher poses: What do you think was the original subtraction problem?

Kristen records 625 – 272 and shares her expression with a partner.

The teacher solicits different expressions reinforcing that each has the difference of 353. The teacher reveals her Partial Sums problem and celebrates with the class if anyone has created the same problem. In this example, the teacher's problem was 615 – 262. The teacher might then have students compare and contrast their expression with the teacher's, noting how certain place values are similar.

ACTIVITY 3.7

Name: "Complex Number Strings"   **Type:** Routine

About the Routine: Students benefit from opportunities to practice adding multiples of 10, 100, or 1,000 that are related to a specific basic fact. This routine helps students see patterns in problems with related addends while also reinforcing connections to basic facts.

Materials: series of related expressions

Directions:
1. Provide a matrix of related number strings with one known sum.

2. Students use the known sum to work across the rows and down the columns.

3. After students signal that they know the sums of each, you hold a class discussion about how the first known relates to the others. You want to draw students' attention to how adding the ones relates to the number of tens, hundreds, and thousands. Keep in mind that you want to remind students that they aren't adding a zero each time but instead are thinking about the number of tens, hundreds, or thousands that were added.

9 + 7 = 16	90 + 70 =	900 + 700 =	9,000 + 7,000 =
9 + 6 =	90 + 60 =	900 + 600 =	9,000 + 6,000 =
9 + 3 =	90 + 30 =	900 + 300 =	9,000 + 3,000 =
9 + 2 =	90 + 20 =	900 + 200 =	9,000 + 2,000 =

TEACHING TAKEAWAY

Remind students they aren't adding a zero each time but instead are thinking about the number of tens, hundreds, or thousands that were added.

It might seem a bit overwhelming to create all of these problems, but it's much easier than you might think. To start, think of a basic fact (9 + 7 = 16). Create a row of related problems with increasing place values (90 + 70, 900 + 700, etc.). Then, create some problems just below the basic fact that is related in some way (an addend is one more or one less, half, and so on). Then, create rows for each of the new basic facts in a similar way for the original basic fact.

ACTIVITY 3.8

Name: "Too Much Taken???"   **Type:** Routine

About the Routine: Using Partial Differences can be challenging because there are situations where we encounter a negative amount. In the problem 614 – 182, the partial difference of 10 – 80 is –70. In a different setting, one would regroup a hundred so that the negative is avoided. Understanding the negative result, why it occurs, and how it is used is essential for this strategy. Students *can* do this. In this routine, students practice taking away too much.

Materials: This routine does not require any materials.

Directions: 1. Pose a few related equations.

2. Have students determine if they think the equations are true or false.

3. Conclude the routine by asking students, "How do you know when there will be 'too much' taken?"

Note the relationship across each row. This is intentional and can help you focus the conversation on this relationship. Also note that each row doesn't take too much away. This too is intentional, as we don't want to inadvertently "teach" students to always have a negative amount.

Example 1 →	$5 - 7 = -2$	$50 - 70 = -20$	$500 - 700 = -200$
Example 2 →	$9 - 6 = 3$	$90 - 60 = 30$	$900 - 600 = 300$
Example 3 →	$3 - 8 = -5$	$30 - 80 = -50$	$300 - 800 = -500$
Example 4 →	$7 - 3 = 4$	$70 - 30 = -40$	$700 - 300 = 400$

ACTIVITY 3.9

Name: For Keeps   **Type:** Game

About the Game: *For Keeps* is an opportunity to practice adding or subtracting in an engaging way that also helps students develop reasoning about numbers. The goal is to keep two sums that will have a sum greater than an opponent's sum of sums.

Materials: *For Keeps* game board, 10-sided dice or digit cards (0–9) or playing cards (queens = 0, aces = 1, kings and jacks removed)

Directions: 1. By rolling the die or drawing cards, players generate four numbers and make 2 two-digit addends.

2. Players find the sum of the two addends and decide if they want to keep the sum as the score for the round or if they don't want to keep it for a score. Once they decide (before the next problem), the decision is final and the sum can't be moved later.

3. Players play a total of four rounds yet can only keep two of those rounds. At the end of the fourth round, each player adds the two scores that they kept.

4. The player with the higher score wins.

In the following example, the player first made 22 + 31 for a sum of 53 that wasn't kept for points. The second sum of 139 was kept and the player thinks they can do better than 94 in the fourth round. No matter what sum is made in the fourth round, the player will have to keep it. The sum of the two kept scores (139 and the fourth round) will be the player's score.

Round	Numbers Created		Sum For Keeps	Sum and NOT Kept
1	22	31		53
2	68	71	139	
3	44	50		94
4				
	Sum of Keeps			

RESOURCE(S) FOR THIS ACTIVITY

For Keeps

Directions: Make two two-digit numbers. Find the sum and decide if you want to keep the sum as a score or not keep it. You can only keep two of the four rounds. After the fourth round, add the two scores you kept. The player with the higher score wins.

Round	Numbers Created		Sum For Keeps	Sum and NOT Kept
1				
2				
3				
4				
	Sum of Keeps			

1	2	3	4
5	6	7	8
9	1	2	3
4	5	6	7
8	9	0	0

online resources Digit cards and this game board can be downloaded at **resources.corwin.com/FOF/ addsubtractwholenumber**.

ACTIVITY 3.10

Name: Sum Duel   **Type:** Game

About the Game: *Sum Duel* is a unique way to practice adding with partials. Players make sums and earn points for each condition their sum or difference matches.

Materials: *Sum Duel* game board per player, two-sided counters, *Sum Duel* condition cards

Directions:

1. Player 1 puts four chips (white chips in the example) on the board to show a decomposed four-digit number and records the number.

2. The player then puts four chips (gray chips in the example) on the board to show another decomposed four-digit number and the player records the number.

3. The player adds the two recorded numbers 8,667 (white chips) and 3,758 (gray chips) using the Partial Sums strategy.

4. This is repeated for the other player.

5. The players then turn over *Sum Duel* cards and get a point for each condition their sum matches.

6. The first player to 5 points wins the game.

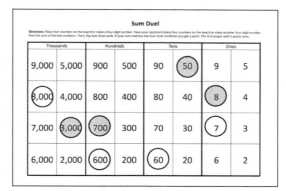

RESOURCE(S) FOR THIS ACTIVITY

Largest sum	Smallest sum	Even sum
Odd sum	Sum with a 7 in it	Sum with a 9 in it
Sum with two digits that are the same	Sum with a 4 in it	Sum with an 8 in it

Sum with exactly 5 tens	Sum with 3 tens	Sum with 5 or more hundreds
Sum with two 8s in it	Sum with two 4s in it	Sum greater than 5,000
Sum with three digits that are the same	Sum with two 5s in it	Sum without any 2s in it

Sum Duel

Thousands		Hundreds		Tens		Ones	
9,000	5,000	900	500	90	50	9	5
8,000	4,000	800	400	80	40	8	4
7,000	3,000	700	300	70	30	7	3
6,000	2,000	600	200	60	20	6	2

online resources Condition cards and this game board can be downloaded at **resources.corwin.com/FOF/ addsubtractwholenumber**.

ACTIVITY 3.11

Name: 100 or 0   **Type:** Game

About the Game: In *100 or 0*, students practice both addition and subtraction. The goal of each round is to get as close to the target as possible (100 if adding, 0 if subtracting). You can change the addition target to 1,000 for adding three-digit addends or 10,000 for adding four-digit addends.

Materials: one 2-color counter (or coin), digit cards (0–9) or playing cards (queens = 0, aces = 1, kings and jacks removed), *100 or 0* game board

Directions:
1. Players each get four digit cards to create 2 two-digit numbers.

2. A player flips the two-sided counter to see if they will add or subtract (like flipping a coin).

3. Players then arrange their cards to make numbers that get close to 100 (if adding) or to 0 (if subtracting).

4. The player closest to 100 or 0 gets a point. The first to 5 points wins.

TEACHING TAKEAWAY

Games can be modified to be used as centers and centers can be adjusted to be played as games.

The recording sheet provides an example of how the game is played. The player pulls digit cards of 4, 7, 3, and 4. They flip to determine that they will be adding for a target of 100. Then, the player makes 44 + 37 for a sum of 81 showing their work with Partial Sums. The player was not closest to 100 (their opponent has 94, *not shown*).

RESOURCE(S) FOR THIS ACTIVITY

100 or 0

Directions: Pull four cards. Flip a counter or coin to see if you will add or subtract. Use your four cards to make 2 two-digit numbers that are close to 100 (if adding) or close to 0 (if subtracting). The player closest to 100 or 0 wins a point. The first player to earn 5 points wins the game.

My Numbers	+ or −	My problem	Closest to 100 or 0
4, 7, 3, 4	+	44 + 37 4 + 7 = 11 44 + 37 = 81 40 + 30 = 70	No

1	2	3	4
5	6	7	8
9	1	2	3
4	5	6	7
8	9	0	0

online resources ↘ Digit cards and this game board can be downloaded at **resources.corwin.com/FOF/ addsubtractwholenumber**.

ACTIVITY 3.12

Name: Partial Concentration   **Type:** Game

About the Game: *Partial Concentration* helps students think about how partial sums and differences are used to solve expressions. Students work to match problems with partial sum recordings of the problem.

Materials: deck of *Partial Concentration* cards

Directions: This game is played similarly to a traditional game of memory or concentration.

1. Players place cards face down in an array.

2. Players take turns flipping over cards attempting to match an expression with a card that shows how to solve the problem with the Partial Sums and Differences strategy.

3. The player who makes the most matches wins the game.

A set of *Partial Concentration* cards is available for download. Note that you can also create your own set of partial index cards.

RESOURCE(S) FOR THIS ACTIVITY

$249 - 138$	$200 - 100 = 100$ $40 - 30 = 10$ $9 - 8 = 1$ $100 + 10 + 1 = 111$	$294 - 183$	$200 - 100 = 100$ $90 - 80 = 10$ $4 - 3 = 1$ $100 + 10 + 1 = 111$
$538 - 317$	$500 - 300 = 200$ $30 - 10 = 20$ $8 - 7 = 1$ $200 + 20 + 1 = 221$	$587 - 313$	$500 - 300 = 200$ $80 - 10 = 70$ $7 - 3 = 4$ $200 + 70 + 4 = 274$
$625 - 415$	$600 - 400 = 200$ $20 - 10 = 10$ $5 - 5 = 0$ $200 + 10 + 0 = 210$	$626 - 415$	$600 - 400 = 200$ $20 - 10 = 10$ $6 - 5 = 1$ $200 + 10 + 1 = 211$
$375 - 22$	$300 - 0 = 300$ $70 - 20 = 50$ $5 - 2 = 3$ $300 + 50 + 3 = 353$	$357 - 27$	$300 - 0 = 300$ $50 - 20 = 30$ $7 - 7 = 0$ $300 + 30 + 1 = 330$
$864 - 487$	$800 - 400 = 400$ $60 - 80 = -20$ $4 - 7 = -3$ $400 - 20 - 3 = 377$	$524 - 137$	$500 - 100 = 400$ $20 - 30 = -10$ $4 - 7 = -3$ $400 - 10 - 3 = 387$

online resources — This resource can be downloaded at **resources.corwin.com/FOF/addsubtractwholenumber**.

ACTIVITY 3.13

Name: Partial Sums With Ten-Frames and Place Value Disks

Type: Center

About the Center: Place value disks are a good alternative to base-10 blocks when students are comfortable with nonproportional models. They can be used in conjunction with ten-frames to show expanded form and to help students make sense of regrouping. This center is a practice opportunity for decomposing a number by place value and then adding to find partials. This center is a good choice for early learning about the Partial Sums and Partial Differences strategy.

Materials: place value ten-frame mats, place value disks, recording sheet

Directions: 1. A student scoops a pile of place value disks.

2. The student sorts the pile and places the disks on the place value ten-frame mat.

3. The student records the number on a recording sheet or in their journal.

4. The student scoops another pile of place value disks, sorts them, and arranges them on a second mat.

5. The student records the second number and then finds the sum of the two numbers by using the Partial Sums strategy.

6. The student can use the place value disks to help them add place values.

A ten-frame place value mat is available for download. Other versions for two- and three-digit numbers are also available. You can also join a ones through thousands ten-frame mat with a ten-thousands through ten-millions mat for work with even larger numbers. Keep in mind that many strategies lose efficiency with such large addends.

Student collects and sorts her place value disks.	
Student puts her place value disks on the ten-frame place value mat.	
Student records the number she made (3,689).	

3,689

Student collects and sorts her place value disks. Student puts her place value disks on the ten-frame place value mat. Student records the second number she made (6,129).	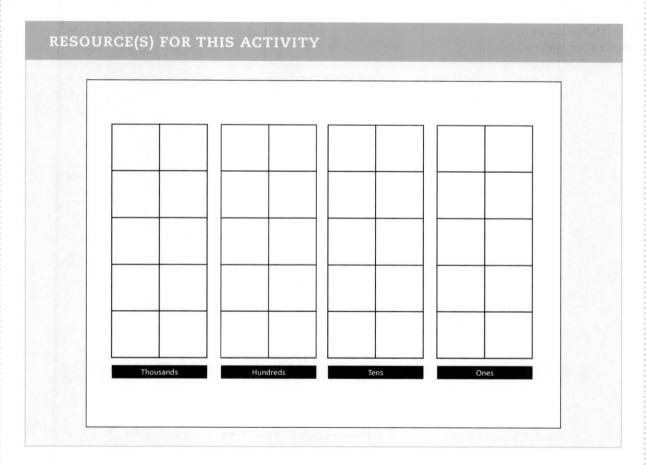 6,129
The student then finds the sum of these two numbers using Partial Sums.	3,000 + 6,000 = 9,000 600 + 100 = 700 80 + 20 = 100 9 + 9 = 18 3,689 + 6,129 = 9,818

RESOURCE(S) FOR THIS ACTIVITY

Thousands	Hundreds	Tens	Ones

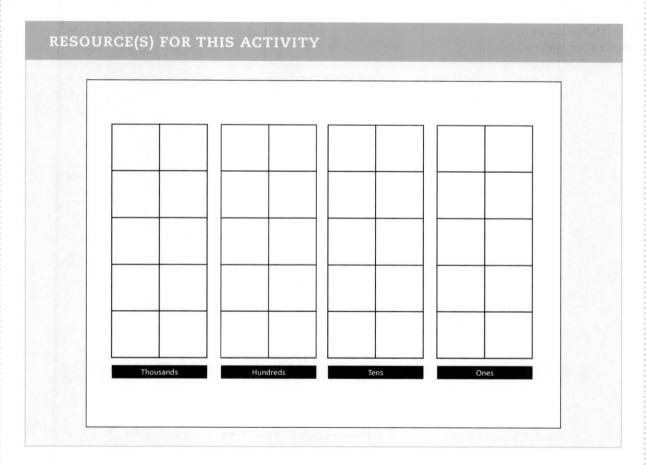

online resources This resource can be downloaded at **resources.corwin.com/FOF/addsubtractwholenumber**.

ACTIVITY 3.14

Name: Target 1,000   **Type:** Center

About the Center: Target sums and differences games are dynamic opportunities for practice. In this center, students create three-digit addends with a sum as close to 1,000 as possible.

Materials: two decks of digit cards (0–9) or playing cards (queens = 0, aces = 1, kings and jacks removed), Target 1,000 recording sheet

Directions:
1. Students pull three digit cards to make a three-digit addend.

2. Students pull three more digit cards to make another three-digit addend.

3. Students arrange the digits in each to create two addends with a sum as close to 1,000 as possible.

4. Students add the numbers with Partial Sums to show how close their sum is to 1,000.

TEACHING TAKEAWAY

To save paper, print recording sheets and put them in plastic sleeves or laminate them and have students use dry-erase markers.

You can easily adjust this game in a variety of ways. You can set a target of 100 for finding three-digit differences or two-digit sums, or a target of 10,000 for adding four-digit numbers. But you also might, in time, think about having more novel targets to enrich the activity. For example, you might set a target of 500 or 750 for 2 three-digit numbers.

RESOURCE(S) FOR THIS ACTIVITY

Target 1,000

Directions: Pull three digit cards to make a number. Pull three more digit cards to make another problem. Arrange the digits in each number so that the sum of the two numbers is as close to 1,000 as possible. Use partial sums to find the sum of the two numbers.

Digits for my first number	Digits for my second number	Addition problem I created	How I added the numbers with partial sums

online resources — Digit cards and this recording sheet can be downloaded at **resources.corwin.com/FOF/addsubtractwholenumber**.

Notes

Compensation Strategy

STRATEGY OVERVIEW:
Compensation

What is Compensation? This strategy involves adjusting the expression to make it easier to add, and then compensating (either before or after you compute) to preserve equivalence. The quantities tend to be rounded up to a convenient number (a benchmark), and then an opposite move is made to ensure the answer is correct. Consider the following two strategies to add the basic fact of 9 + 6.

MAKING 10	PRETEND-A-10 (COMPENSATION)
1. Notice that 9 is 1 away from 10.	1. Pretend the 9 *is a* 10.
2. Decompose 6 into 1 + 5.	2. Add 10 + 6: 10 + 6 = 16.
3. "Give" 1 to the 9, rethinking the expression as 10 + 5.	3. Compensate by subtracting 1: 16 – 1 = 15.
4. Add 10 + 5 = 15.	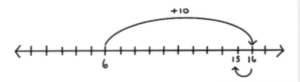

HOW DOES COMPENSATION WORK FOR ADDITION?

This strategy is the zero property in action. If 3 is added to an addend to add, then 3 is subtracted from the sum: 197 + 435 [add 3] → 200 + 435 → 635 [subtract 3] → 632. There are often many ways to compensate, as a person looks for convenient numbers to add, as illustrated by these examples:

Problem: 37 + 38

Change both to 40

Add 40 + 40 = 80

Compensate: added 5 too much, so subtract 5: 75

Problem: 497 + 1,258

Change 497 to 500

Add 500 + 1,258 = 1,758

Compensate: added 3 too much, so subtract 3: 1,755

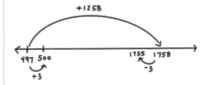

Problem: 424 + 379

Add 420 + 380 = 800

Compensate: subtracted 4 and added 1, so net change was subtract 3; need to add 3: 80

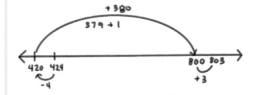

Problem: 6,245 + 3,379

Change 3,379 to 3,400

Add 6,245 + 3,400 = 9,645

Compensate: added 21 too much, so subtract 21: 9,624

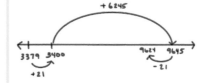

HOW DOES COMPENSATION WORK FOR SUBTRACTION?

Compensation when subtracting "behaves" differently than when adding, and attention must be given to *which* number is being changed. Consider 63 – 38. Adding to the minuend (63) means *adding* extra (so to compensate, that quantity will later be subtracted). Adding to the subtrahend (38) means *subtracting* extra (so to compensate, that quantity will later be added).

OPTION 1: CHANGE THE MINUEND (START NUMBER)	OPTION 2: CHANGE THE SUBTRAHEND (SECOND NUMBER)
Problem: 63 – 38	**Problem: 63 – 38**
Change: 63 to 68	Change: 38 to 40
Solve: 68 – 38 = 30	Solve: 63 – 40 = 23
Compensate: added 5 too much, so subtract 5: 25	Compensate: subtracted 2 too much, so must add 2: 25
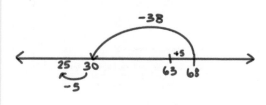	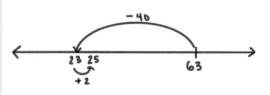

Subtraction is not only take away but also finding the difference (compare). The compare interpretation gives us access to a great way to compensate—a slide on the number line. The difference or distance between 38 and 63 is the same if we add 2 to both numbers and look for the difference between 40 and 65, which is 25. This is Compensation because you are adding 2 into the problem and compensating by also taking 2 away (by increasing the subtrahend by 2).

> **TEACHING TAKEAWAY**
>
> The compare interpretation of subtraction leads to a great way to use the Compensation strategy.

Option 3: Change Both (slide on the number line)

Problem: 63 – 38

Change: 38 to 40 (it is easier to subtract 40)

Compensate: 63 to 65 (maintain same difference)

Solve: 65 – 40 = 25

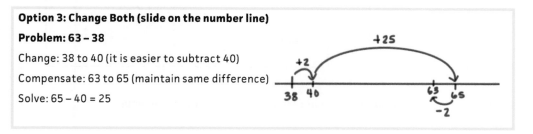

This applies to larger values as well. For 721 – 488, think, "What can I add to both to have a convenient subtrahend? (12)." Hence, 721 – 488 = 733 – 500. The answer is 233. Students often want to focus on rounding the minuend, but with experience, they will see that rounding the subtrahend usually works better.

WHEN DO YOU CHOOSE COMPENSATION?

This strategy is very versatile, so it works well in almost any problem adding or subtracting within 1,000, particularly when one or both numbers are near a benchmark. It is also useful in subtraction situations that involve regrouping because it is an efficient way to get an answer and avoid the common pitfalls of regrouping.

MODULE 1 Count On/Count Back

MODULE 2 Make Tens Strategy

MODULE 3 Partial Sums and Differences Strategy

MODULE 4 Compensation Strategy

MODULE 5 Think Addition Strategy

MODULE 6 Standard Algorithms for Addition and Subtraction

COMPENSATION:
Strategy Briefs for Families

It is important that families understand the strategies and know how they work so that they can be partners in the pursuit of fluency. These strategy briefs are a tool for doing that. You can include them in parent or school newsletters or share them at parent conferences. They are available for download so that you can adjust them as needed.

Compensation Strategy for Addition

How It Works: We can adjust numbers to make them easier to add. After we add the easier numbers, we can "undo" our adjustment.

1. Identify an easier problem.
2. Modify the original problem.
3. Solve the new problem.
4. Compensate for how the original problem was modified.

The left example shows that 37 + 38 can be thought of as 40 + 40. We would add 3 to 37 to make it 40. Then we would add 2 to 38 to make it 40. When you combine the 40 + 40, it is an easier problem to add: 40 + 40 = 80. We added 5 (3 and 2) to make the easier problem, so we have to take away that 5 from 80.

The right example shows that for 497 + 1,258, we thought of 497 as 500. We added 500 + 1,258. Then we took 3 away.

When It's Useful: This strategy is useful when one number (or both) is near a benchmark.

Addend	Addend
37	+ 38

37 + 38
[+3 +2] -5
40 + 40 = 80
80 [-5] = 75

Addend	Addend
497	+ 1,258

497 + 1,258
[+3]
500 + 1,258 = 1,758
1,758 [-3] = 1,755

Compensation Strategy for Subtraction

How It Works: We can adjust numbers to make them easier to subtract. After we subtract the easier numbers, we can "undo" our adjustment.

1. Identify an easier problem.
2. Modify the original problem.
3. Solve the new problem.
4. Compensate for how the original problem was modified.

The left example shows that 63 − 38 can be thought of as 68 − 38, which is 30. 68 is 5 more than 63, so the difference of 30 is 5 more than the difference of the original problem (63 − 38). Or you can think of 63 − 38 as 63 − 40, which is 23.

The right example shows that we took 2 too much away so we have to "put it back." 23 + 2 is 25. So, the original problem 63 − 38 = 25.

When It's Useful: This strategy is useful when one number (or both) is near a benchmark. It is also useful instead of regrouping.

Minuend	Subtrahend
63	− 38

63 − 38
[+5]
68 + 38 = 30
30 [-5] = 25

Minuend	Subtrahend
63	− 38

63 − 38
[+2]
63 − 40 = 23
23 [+2] = 25

 These resources can be downloaded at **resources.corwin.com/FOF/addsubtractwholenumber**.

NOTES

_____

_____

_____

TEACHING ACTIVITIES for Compensation

Before students are able to choose strategies, a key to fluency, they first must be able to understand and use relevant strategies. These activities focus on using Compensation to add and subtract. While students may employ other methods, which is appropriate, they must understand how this strategy works, be able to implement it mentally, and become familiar with examples of problems in which they will want to use it.

ACTIVITY 4.1
ESTABLISHING COMPENSATION THROUGH LENGTH

It is critical to establish that compensation, when done correctly, does indeed yield the same sum. It is wise to first do this with somewhat simplistic addends so that you can take advantage of physical models. Using linking cubes, show that you can adjust 9 + 6 to 10 + 6, and then adjust the sum.

9 + 6 = ?

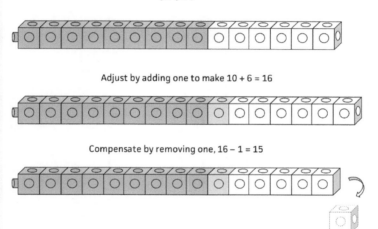

Adjust by adding one to make 10 + 6 = 16

Compensate by removing one, 16 − 1 = 15

TEACHING TAKEAWAY

Start by using simplistic addends to establish that compensation, when done correctly, does use the same sum.

This example is a basic fact that some students might already know. Because of this, they may not process the idea of adjusting the addends because they simply know both facts. It is critical that you focus their attention on how the expressions change by giving some from one addend to another. As students show understanding of compensation with single-digit addends, begin to expose them to larger addends but keep in mind that it's best to focus on sums to 30 at first so that tools like linking cubes remain viable. Begin to pose problems like 29 + 9, asking students to adjust one or both addends focusing attention on the different ways an expression can be adjusted and the ways that result in the most efficient computations. For example, 29 + 9 might be thought of as 29 + 10 (then remove 1 after adding), 30 + 9 (then remove 1 after adding), or 30 + 10 (then remove 2 after adding). The linking cubes physically show the extra cube(s) that are removed to maintain equivalence.

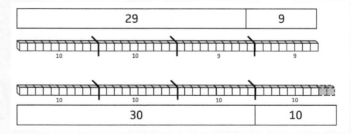

This work can be accompanied by bar models (as shown) and equations. This will be helpful as three-digit numbers are introduced in later grades.

ACTIVITY 4.2
THE JUMPS HAVE IT

A Hundred Chart is a good tool for proving if a Compensation strategy yields the same result if applied correctly. In this activity, pose a prompt like "28 + 36 is the same as" and record it on the board. Ask students to generate different ways the addends might be adjusted. Record some of their expressions. Record the sum of the original problem (28 + 36 = 64). Then, have students use the Hundred Chart to determine which of the other expressions have the same sum. After confirming the expressions that have the same sum, discuss with students which adjusted expressions make the original problem the most efficient to think about.

In this example, a student shares that 28 + 36 is the same as 28 + 40 and then take 4 away. She proves that her thinking is the same as she makes a jump of 40 (to 68) and jumps back 4 to 64. The teacher records her thinking and asks for other ideas.

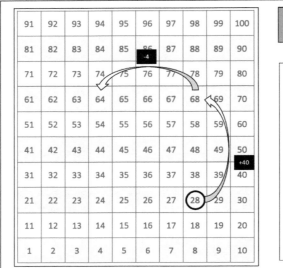

Another student shares that he thought of 28 + 36 as 30 + 40 and then he jumped back 6. His thinking is evident in the chart on the left and the recording on the right.

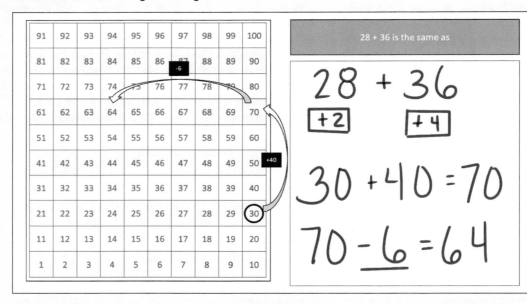

ACTIVITY 4.3
ADJUSTING ONE OR BOTH?

As the examples in Activity 4.2 illustrate, with addition, students can adjust one or more addends to make the adding more convenient. They need to keep track of what they are adjusting so they can later compensate. The decision of whether to change one or to change both addends is dependent on the numbers and the person. Help students consider the options and decide how they want to add. For this activity, pose a problem such as 37 + 38. Have students adjust one number (their choice), add, and compensate. For example, 40 + 38 – 3. Then, have students adjust both numbers to 40, find the sum, and then compensate (40 + 40 – 5). Invite students to discuss which way they like. Pose another example, such as 51 + 47. Repeat the process.

The following reproducible can be used to record student thinking. Any problems will work. Some to consider include the following:

TWO-DIGIT ADDITION	TWO-DIGIT AND THREE-DIGIT ADDITION	THREE-DIGIT ADDITION	FOUR-DIGIT ADDITION
47 + 48	636 + 28	199 + 199	3,379 + 6,245
36 + 28	546 + 38	424 + 317	2,497 + 1,258
53 + 69	122 + 59	205 + 766	4,288 + 2,016

Note that this can be extended to adding more than two addends: for example, 48 + 29 + 31 or 89 + 38 + 67 + 19.

RESOURCE(S) FOR THIS ACTIVITY

47 + 48	122 + 59
36 + 28	636 + 28
58 + 69	546 + 38
67 + 28	205 + 66
97 + 27	357 + 135

Adjust One or Both?

Directions: Record an addition problem. In the middle column, show a way to adjust one addend. In the right column, show how to adjust both numbers.

Original Problem	Adjusting One Addend	Adjust Both Addends
37 + 38	37 + 40 = 77 (add 2 to 38) 77 – 2 = 75 (compensate) OR 40 + 38 = 78 (add 3 to 37) 78 – 3 = 75 (compensate)	40 + 40 = 80 (add 3 to 37 and 2 to 38) 80 – 5 = 75 (compensate)

52 – 19	122 – 89
74 – 49	776 – 28
46 – 27	365 – 19
63 – 38	57 – 38
48 – 19	265 – 29

online resources 🖦 This resource can be downloaded at **resources.corwin.com/FOF/addsubtractwholenumber**.

ACTIVITY 4.4
GENERALIZE AND JUSTIFY

As you have read, there are options for how to compensate with subtraction. Adjusting the minuend (starting number) "behaves" more like compensation with addition (if you adjust by adding 3, you later subtract by subtracting 3). Adjusting the subtrahend, however, "behaves" differently. Consider how the Compensation strategy "works" in these two situations when 29 is adjusted to 30:

	56 + 29	56 – 29
Adjust:	56 + 30 (add 1)	56 – 30 (add 1)
Compute:	86	26
Compensate	**85 (subtract 1)**	**27 (add 1)**

In the case of adjusting the subtrahend, if you add something, it means you are taking away more than the original problem, so you have to *add* it back to the answer.

This activity can be implemented first with a focus on the minuend, and second with a focus on the subtrahend (or they can be mixed). Pose a series of three to five problems and ask students to adjust (e.g., the subtrahend), subtract, and compensate. Then ask,

● What did you notice across these problems?

● What generalization can we make (in words)?

● How can we justify our generalization?

Give students time in groups to prepare a justification. A justification can involve counters, number lines, or generalized situations (e.g., "When I added 1, it was like I took out one extra dollar so I had to put that dollar back in"). The examples here lend to changing the subtrahend (it is close to a benchmark).

TWO-DIGIT SUBTRACTION	TWO-DIGIT AND THREE-DIGIT SUBTRACTION	THREE-DIGIT SUBTRACTION	FOUR-DIGIT SUBTRACTION
52 – 19	122 – 89	192 – 138	2,014 – 1,020
74 – 49	776 – 28	351 – 204	3,028 – 2,059
46 – 27	365 – 19	571 – 388	4,031 – 3,015

ACTIVITY 4.5
METER STICK COMPENSATION (CONSTANT DIFFERENCE)

This activity focuses on a third way to compensate: changing both numbers in a way that keeps the difference the same. Students work to show how the difference between two numbers remains constant using a meter stick. Meter sticks make excellent number lines. Using centimeters, they show 0 to 100. You can put multiple meter sticks together to show numbers greater than 100. To begin, have students work in small groups, sharing a meter stick and objects to measure. Those objects might include crayons, pencils, books, or erasers (or they could measure paper strips made from colored construction paper). Each student chooses an item, measures it using the meter stick, and records the measurement (e.g., 7 cm). Then, students find other spaces on the meter stick that have the same difference and record those distances (differences).

For example, a group chooses a crayon that has a length of 7 cm. They place it on the meter stick, noting that the difference of 38 and 45 is 7 (recording 45 – 38). They slide the crayon to the right or left until they find a "friendly" subtrahend, such as sliding up 2 to show the distance 47 – 40 (and recording 45 – 38 = 47 – 40). After students engage in the exploration, facilitate a discussion where students explain why 65 – 58 is the same as 67 – 60 and why that is useful to know.

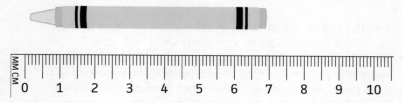

The crayon is 7 cm.

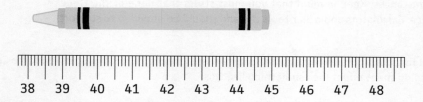

The crayon is 7 cm. The difference of 45 and 38 is 7: 45 – 38 = 7.

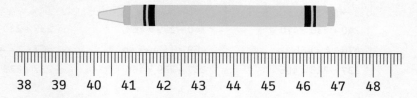

The crayon is 7 cm. The difference between 47 and 40 is the same as 45 and 38.

Source: Crayon image from iStock/ksana-gribakina

 ACTIVITY 4.6
THREE FOR ME

When subtracting, you can adjust three different ways, changing the first number, the second number, or both numbers. These are choices. Students need to understand this and that no one approach is *the* approach to compensation. As students learned in Activity 4.5, *how* you compensate depends on which number you adjust. This activity provides an opportunity for students to explore options for the same problems.

For example, we can compensate for 63 – 38 in three different ways.

ORIGINAL PROBLEM	TAKE TOO MUCH AWAY THEN ADD IT BACK	ADD ON THEN TAKE IT BACK	ADJUST BOTH NUMBERS
63 – 38	63 – 40 = 23 23 + 2 = 25, so 63 – 38 = 25	68 – 38 = 30 30 – 5 = 25, so 63 – 38 = 25	Give 2 to both. 65 – 40 = 25, so 63 – 38 = 25

We can compensate for subtracting three- and four-digit numbers such as the following:

ORIGINAL PROBLEM	TAKE TOO MUCH AWAY THEN ADD IT BACK	ADD ON THEN TAKE IT BACK	ADJUST BOTH NUMBERS
571 − 388	571 − 400 = 171 171 + 12 = 183, so 571 − 388 = 183	588 − 388 = 200 200 − 17 = 183, so 571 − 388 = 183	Give 12 to both. 583 − 400 = 183, so 571 − 388 = 183

In this activity, partners work to apply the strategy to subtraction problems in three different ways. They should record their thinking on a recording sheet that looks like the tables on the previous page. They can fold a piece of notebook paper in half and in half again to create the four columns or you can download the reproducible. After working two or three problems, the group comes back together to share their findings. At this time, it is important that you focus on the similarities and differences between these approaches. You also want students to begin to identify which compensation approach they prefer and for which circumstances. Keep in mind that you must stress that none of the three are the correct choice. Calculators and other tools can and should be provided to support student accuracy.

Three for Me is used for subtraction in this activity. You can easily modify it to develop or reinforce Compensation with addition. That recording sheet might look something like this:

	ADD EXTRA TO BOTH ADDENDS THEN TAKE IT BACK	ADD EXTRA TO FIRST ADDEND THEN TAKE IT BACK	ADD EXTRA TO THE SECOND ADDEND THEN TAKE IT BACK
237 + 229	240 + 230 = 470 470 − 4 = 466, so 237 + 229 = 466	240 + 229 = 469 469 − 3 = 466, so 237 + 229 = 466	237 + 230 = 467 467 − 1 = 466, so 237 + 229 = 466

RESOURCE(S) FOR THIS ACTIVITY

This resource can be downloaded at **resources.corwin.com/FOF/addsubtractwholenumber**.

ACTIVITY 4.7 PROMPTS FOR TEACHING COMPENSATION

Use the following prompts as opportunities to develop understanding of, and reasoning with, the strategy. Have students use representations and tools to justify their thinking, including base-10 models, number lines, number charts, and so on. After students work with the prompt(s), bring the class together to exchange ideas. These could be useful for collecting evidence of student understanding. Any prompt can be easily modified to feature different numbers (e.g., three-digit or four-digit numbers) and any prompt can be offered more than once if modified.

• Makenna changed 37 + 58 into 40 + 60. What does she have to do next to find the sum of the original problem?

• Jenni thought to add 27 + 28 as 30 + 30 and then took 5 away. Connie added 30 + 28 and then took 3 away. Did Jenni and Connie have the same sum?

• Avery is working with 365 – 219. She says it's easier to think about it as 366 – 220. Why do you think Avery thinks this is an easier problem? Does it always work?

• Marlon says you can solve 398 + 600 using Compensation, changing the expression to 498 + 500. Do you agree or disagree that 398 + 600 is a good "fit" for compensation?

• Susie says that 48 + 59 could be adjusted in two different ways. What do you think she means?

• Krissy has to add 671 + 1,347. She thinks it's easier to add 675 + 1,350 instead of 671 + 1,347. Do you agree with Krissy? What does she have to do next if she adds the easier problem?

• Explain how you know that 744 – 388 is the same as 756 – 400.

• Jake solved 744 – 388 by thinking 744 – 400. What do you think he did next?

• How is adding 42 + 38 like adding 42 + 40? How is it different?

• Mrs. Morris found three different ways students were solving 43 + 38.

   ○ Rosalie solved it 43 + 38 → 40 + 40 = 80 → 80 + 1 = 81.

   ○ Thomas solved it 40 + 38 = 78 → 78 + 3 = 81.

   ○ Adriana solved it 43 + 40 = 83 → 83 – 2 = 81.

   How are the students' strategies the same? How are they different?

NOTES

_____

_____

_____

_____

_____

PRACTICE ACTIVITIES for Compensation

Fluency is realized through quality practice that is focused, varied, processed, and connected. The activities in this section focus students' attention on how this strategy works and when to use it. The activities are a collection of varied engagements. The discussion you facilitate after an activity or the reflection prompts you attach to it should help students think about what they did mathematically, how they reasoned about the activity, and when the math they did (namely the strategy) might be useful. Debriefing should also help students see how the practice activity connects to recent instruction or how the strategy connects to other strategies they know. Game boards, recording sheets, digit cards, and other required materials are available as online resources for you to download, possibly modify, and use. As students work with activities, you want to look for how well they are acquiring the strategy and assimilating it into their collection of strategies.

FLUENCY COMPONENT	WHAT TO LOOK FOR AS STUDENTS PRACTICE THIS STRATEGY
Efficiency	• Are students using the Compensation strategy or are they reverting to previously learned and/or possibly less appropriate strategies? • Are students using the Compensation strategy efficiently? (e.g., 483 – 319 may be more efficiently solved with compensation by using 484 – 320 instead of 499 – 335.) • Do they use the Compensation regardless of its appropriateness for the problem at hand? (Compensation likely isn't efficient for problems like 561 – 400 or 561 – 460.)
Flexibility	• Are students carrying out Compensation in flexible ways (i.e., sometimes changing one addend, sometimes changing both)? • Do they change their approach to or from this compensation as it proves inappropriate or overly complicated for the problem? (e.g., Do they change to compensation as they start to decompose 406 + 799 for finding partial sums?)
Accuracy	• Are students using the Compensation strategy when adding accurately (giving from one addend to another)? • Are students compensating accurately when subtracting (finding constant difference)? • Are they estimating the sum/difference? • Are students finding accurate solutions? • Are they considering the reasonableness of their solutions?*

*This consideration is not unique to this strategy and should be practiced throughout the pursuit of fluency with whole numbers.

WORKED EXAMPLES

Worked examples are problems that have been solved. Correctly worked examples can help students make sense of a strategy and incorrectly worked examples attend to common errors.

As you have read throughout this module, Compensation has *options* and this strategy *works differently* for addition and subtraction. Hence, worked examples are important for helping students make sense of Compensation and implement it accurately. Common challenges or errors when using Compensation include the following:

1. The student applies an idea that works for addition to a subtraction problem.
   • 58 – 29: changes the problem to 57 – 30, "moving one over" [using the idea that 58 + 29 = 57 + 30]

2. The student changes the problem but does not compensate for that change.
   - 78 + 44: changes the problem to 80 + 44, adds to get 124, then stops.
   - 479 – 380: changes the problem to 480 – 380, subtracts to get 100, then stops.
3. The student goes the opposite direction in adjusting the answer.
   - 3,249 – 1,980: changes the problem to 3,249 – 2,000, subtracts to get 1,249, and then subtracts 20, instead of adding 20.

The prompts from Activity 4.7 can be used for collecting examples. Throughout the module are various worked examples that you can use as fictional worked examples. A sampling of additional ideas is provided in the following table.

SAMPLE WORKED EXAMPLES FOR COMPENSATION

	ADDITION	SUBTRACTION
Correctly Worked Example (make sense of the strategy) What did _____ do? Why does it work? Is this a good method for this problem?	Yoli's work for 392 + 746: $400 + 746 = 1,146$ $1,146 - 8 = 1,138$	Samuel's work for 3,007 – 1,889: $$\begin{array}{r} 2,999 \\ -\ 1,881 \\ \hline 1,118 \end{array}$$
Partially Worked Example (implement the strategy accurately) Why did _____ start the problem this way? What does _____ need to do to finish the problem?	Cari's start for 8,895 + 6,735: $9,000 + \qquad =$	Teshan's start for 94 – 56: $94 - 54 = 40$
Incorrectly Worked Example (highlight common errors) What did _____ do? What mistake does _____ make? How can this mistake be fixed?	Theo's work for 58 + 45: $$\begin{array}{r} 60 \\ +\ 45 \\ \hline 105 \end{array}$$	Anitria's work for 715 – 322: $715 - 315 = 400$ $400 + 7 = 407$

ACTIVITY 4.8

Name: "Or You Could . . ."   **Type:** Routine

About the Routine: This routine helps students think about how to adjust an expression to create a friendlier problem.

Materials: "Or You Could" cards or other expressions for students to adjust into friendlier problems

Directions: 1. Pose a few expressions to students.

2. Have partners discuss other ways they could think about the problem.

3. Bring the group together to discuss and record the different ways an expression might be thought about. Keep in mind that the point of the routine is not to find the sum or difference but to simply rethink (rewrite) the problem.

4. After recording a few different ideas, prompt students to consider which rewrites are effective in making the problem easier to solve.

For example, you might pose 56 + 98. Students might think about it as 60 + 100 − 6, 54 + 100, 60 + 94, or even 50 + 90 + 6 + 8. After recording these four ideas, you want to discuss with students which is easiest to think about and why. Be careful to avoid inadvertently suggesting there is a certain way that is best.

Expressions to consider for the routine are provided on cards. Keep in mind that *any* expression will work.

RESOURCE(S) FOR THIS ACTIVITY

56 + 98	46 + 49	1,999 + 1,468	6,236 + 4,297	3,362 − 1,297	4,314 − 2,085
24 + 17	88 + 56	2,255 + 1,370	8,345 + 2,198	2,095 − 2,057	3,458 − 1,199
62 + 47	43 + 19	8,015 + 1,095	7,052 + 7,039	5,950 − 1,550	6,287 − 2,065
54 + 79	28 + 22	6,715 + 2,290	5,134 + 3,396	1,562 − 1,299	8,183 − 3,157
33 + 17	22 + 63	5,376 + 4,294	1,999 + 1,999	2,187 − 1,078	9,917 − 8,115

online resources   This resource can be downloaded at **resources.corwin.com/FOF/addsubtractwholenumber**.

ACTIVITY 4.9

Name: "Why Not???"　　　　　　　　　　　　**Type:** Routine

About the Routine: When learning about strategies, students might assume that a strategy is always a good choice for every problem. In other cases, they assume that a problem should be solved with all of the strategies they know. This routine helps them determine if a problem is a good choice for Compensation. Keep in mind that this routine is focused on the Compensation strategy as the only choice.

Materials: prepared expressions for students to consider

Directions:　1. Have students briefly think-pair-share what it means to use the Compensation strategy.

　　2. Pose a few expressions to students.

　　3. Ask partners to consider and discuss which expressions are good choices for solving with a Compensation strategy and which are not.

　　4. Bring the whole group together to share solutions.

For example, you might pose 598 – 200, 363 – 250, 914 – 717, and 524 – 319.

PROBLEM	COMPENSATE? WHY NOT?
598 – 200	No. You can just count back 200 very quickly. 598, 498, 398
363 – 250	No. You can count back in chunks. 363 – 200 then 163 – 50
914 – 717	You could make it 917 – 717 and then take 3 more away because you gave 3 to 914.
524 – 319	Yes. This is probably a good problem for compensation. You could give 1 to each, making 525 – 320, or you could take too much away (320) and then give 1 back.

ACTIVITY 4.10

Name: Who's Adjusting?   **Type:** Game

About the Game: *Who's Adjusting?* helps students practice thinking about when they would adjust a problem and what numbers they would adjust within a problem. The goal is to be the first player to get four in a row.

Materials: expression cards, *Who's Adjusting?* game board for players to share

Directions: 1. Players place the stack of expression cards face down.

2. Players take turns flipping over a problem and deciding how they would adjust the problem.

3. Players put a counter on a space that matches their thinking for the problem.

4. The first player to get four in a row wins.

A deck of playing cards for this game can be created by recording expressions on index cards.

RESOURCE(S) FOR THIS ACTIVITY

Who's Adjusting?

Directions: Players take turns choosing subtraction cards. A player chooses a card and decides if they would adjust before subtracting, adjust after subtracting, adjust the minuend, adjust the subtrahend, or adjust both numbers. The player tells their partner their choice and how they would adjust the problem. The player puts a counter on a space that matches their thinking. The first player to get four-in-a-row wins.

BEFORE	AFTER	MINUEND	SUBTRAHEND	BOTH	AFTER	MINUEND
SUBTRAHEND	BOTH	AFTER	MINUEND	BEFORE	AFTER	MINUEND
BEFORE	AFTER	MINUEND	SUBTRAHEND	BOTH	AFTER	MINUEND
SUBTRAHEND	BOTH	AFTER	MINUEND	BEFORE	AFTER	MINUEND
BEFORE	AFTER	MINUEND	SUBTRAHEND	BOTH	AFTER	MINUEND
SUBTRAHEND	BOTH	AFTER	MINUEND	BEFORE	AFTER	MINUEND
BEFORE	AFTER	MINUEND	SUBTRAHEND	BOTH	AFTER	MINUEND

39 + 78	14 + 77
93 + 22	64 + 67
44 + 88	83 + 17
23 + 86	35 + 19
87 + 14	78 + 13

2,095 − 2,057	3,458 − 1,199
5,950 − 1,550	6,287 − 2,069
1,562 − 1,299	8,183 − 3,157
8,131 − 1,015	9,099 − 2,073
3,495 − 1,157	1,583 − 1,267

online resources → Expression cards and this game board can be downloaded at **resources.corwin.com/FOF/ addsubtractwholenumber**.

ACTIVITY 4.11

Name: *Compensation Concentration*   **Type:** *Game*

About the Game: The matching cards in *Compensation Concentration* focus students' attention on how to rethink expressions using the Compensation strategy. After the game, you can have students choose one of the matches they made and create a new problem that is similar to it.

Materials: *Compensation Concentration* cards

Directions:
1. Players will need expression cards mixed up and laid in rows, face down.

2. Player 1 turns over two cards. If two cards match, the player keeps them. If they don't match, the player turns them back over.

3. Player 2 does the same.

4. Players watch and remember where each card was.

5. The player with the most cards matched at the end is the winner.

TEACHING TAKEAWAY

Have students record their matches on a recording sheet for accountability and an extra dose of practice.

RESOURCE(S) FOR THIS ACTIVITY

Compensation Concentration cards can be downloaded or created with index cards. Possible expressions include the following:

39 + 78	You can think 40 + 80, then remove 3 40 + 80 = 120 120 − 3 = 117	2,999 + 1,459	You can think 3,000 + 1,459, then remove 1 3,000 + 1,459 = 4,459 4,459 − 1 = 4,458
86 + 18	You can think 90 + 20, then remove 6 90 + 20 = 110 110 − 6 = 104	1,148 + 1,152	You can think 1,150 + 1,150
368 + 317	You can think 368 + 320, then remove 3 368 + 320 = 668 668 − 3 = 685	2,219 + 2,125	You can think 2,220 + 2,125, then remove 1 2,220 + 2,125 = 4,345 4,345 − 1 = 4,344
369 + 717	You can think 370 + 720, then remove 4 370 + 720 = 1,090 1,090 − 4 = 1,086	3,314 + 3,319	You can think 3,315 + 3,320, then remove 2 3,315 + 3,320 = 6,635 6,635 − 2 = 6,633
3,015 + 5,174	You can think 3,015 + 5,175, then remove 1 3,015 + 5,175 = 8,190 8,190 − 1 = 8,189	4,536 + 4,217	You can think 4,536 + 4,220, then remove 3 4,536 + 4,220 = 8,756 8,756 − 3 = 8,753

online resources This resource can be downloaded at **resources.corwin.com/FOF/addsubtractwholenumber**.

ACTIVITY 4.12

Name: Compensation Race   **Type:** Game

About the Game: In *Compensation Race*, students practice compensating and using the amount compensated to move their game pieces.

Materials: expression cards, *Compensation Race* game board, and a game piece for each player

Directions: 1. Players take turns choosing an expression card from the deck.

2. The player adjusts the problem to solve the expression.

3. The player advances on the game board by the amount that was adjusted.

4. If a player lands on the same spot as someone else, they lose their next turn.

5. If a player doesn't need to adjust, the player moves to the next closest space with an X.

6. The first player to reach the finish line wins.

Here are some examples:

● A player pulls 38 + 46. The player adjusts the problem by giving 2 to 38 to make the problem 40 + 46. The player moves their game piece 2 spaces. The player could have adjusted it to 38 + 50. If so, that player would have moved 4 spaces instead.

● A player pulls 67 − 39. The player then adjusts it to 67 − 40 and adds 1 back. This player would move 1 space.

● A player pulls 67 + 20. This problem doesn't need to be adjusted because the player can just count on by 2 tens or 20. The player moves to the next space that has an X on it.

RESOURCE(S) FOR THIS ACTIVITY

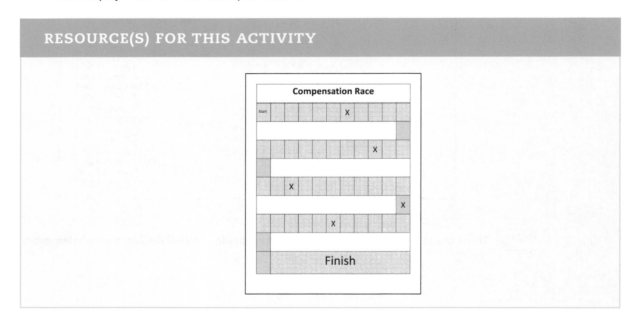

online resources → Expression cards and this game board can be downloaded at **resources.corwin.com/FOF/ addsubtractwholenumber**.

ACTIVITY 4.13

Name: Compensation Lane   **Type:** Center

About the Center: The purpose of this center is for students to practice thinking and recording adjustments they make to solve problems. The Compensation Lane helps them avoid missing the last step where they have to compensate to get the sum or difference.

Materials: expression cards, Compensation Lane recording sheet

Directions: 1. Students select an expression.

2. Students work through the compensation lane to solve the expression.

3. Students record the adjustments they make to solve the problem.

4. Students then compensate for their adjustment (as shown in the example).

RESOURCE(S) FOR THIS ACTIVITY

Compensation Lane

Example   +2   −2

| 46 + 38 | 46 + 40 = 86 | 86 − 2 = 84 |

39 + 78	14 + 77
93 + 22	64 + 67
44 + 88	83 + 17
23 + 86	35 + 19
87 + 14	78 + 13

2,685 + 1,342	3,015 + 5,174
4,322 + 4,388	1,498 + 1,499
2,357 + 3,261	7,618 + 2,220
9,027 + 1,031	2,999 + 1,459
3,074 + 5,115	4,398 + 2,599

2,095 − 2,057	3,458 − 1,199
5,950 − 1,550	6,287 − 2,069
1,562 − 1,299	8,183 − 3,157
8,131 − 1,015	9,099 − 2,073
3,495 − 1,157	1,583 − 1,267

 Center cards and this recording sheet can be downloaded at **resources.corwin.com/FOF/ addsubtractwholenumber**.

ACTIVITY 4.14

Name: *Create Compensations*   **Type:** *Center*

About the Center: Countless problems can be adjusted in very similar ways and even by the same amount. For example, 483 – 229 and 483 – 239 are both likely to be adjusted by the same amount of 1. However, students can develop a misconception that only certain problems can be adjusted by a given amount. This center is a high-order thinking activity for students to create problems that could be adjusted by the given amount. Note that multiple digit cards could be pulled to generate multidigit adjustments. Multidigit adjustments may not always be useful. Students should draw a new number if they can't think of a problem or if the problem they create is not a good problem for adjusting.

Materials: digit cards (0–9), playing cards (queens = 0, aces = 1, kings and jacks removed), or 10-sided dice; Create Compensations recording sheet

Directions: 1. Students generate a number with digit cards or 10-sided dice.

2. Students use the number to generate an expression that they would solve compensating by the amount they generated.

3. Students capture their thinking on the recording sheet.

For example, a player pulls 3. The player creates 365 – 133 because she can think to adjust 133 by 3, creating 365 – 130, and then adds 3 back on.

RESOURCE(S) FOR THIS ACTIVITY

Creating Compensations

Directions: Pull a number. Create a problem that you would adjust by that amount to solve. Record your thinking.

Number I Pulled	Problem I created	How I would adjust it by the number I pulled
3	92 – 37	I can think 92 – 90 and then give 3 back: 92 – 90 = 52 and then 52 + 3 = 55.

1	2	3	4
5	6	7	8
9	1	2	3
4	5	6	7
8	9	0	0

online resources Digit cards and this recording sheet can be downloaded at **resources.corwin.com/FOF/ addsubtractwholenumber.**

ACTIVITY 4.15

Name: Prove It   **Type:** Center

About the Center: Students can confuse how compensation works in different situations. This center helps them reinforce or refine their reasoning about adjusting and compensating.

Materials: Prove It cards and Prove It recording sheet

Directions: 1. A student selects a Prove It card.

2. The student explains that the card is true or false recording their thinking on the recording sheet.

For example, a student pulls a card that says 68 – 31 is the same as 67 – 30. The student then determines that the statement is true because you can take 1 from each and it's the same difference.

> **TEACHING TAKEAWAY**
>
> It is useful to label the cards with a letter so that it is easy to determine the situations that students were working with.

RESOURCE(S) FOR THIS ACTIVITY

81 + 87 is the same as 80 + 88	75 + 28 is the same as 74 + 27
39 + 43 is the same as 40 + 40 and then take away 4	65 + 55 is the same as 77 + 44
390 + 414 is the same as 400 + 404	406 + 721 is the same as 406 + 720 and 1 more
229 + 894 is the same as 229 + 900 and take 6 away	540 + 640 is the same as 550 + 630

Prove It

Directions: Pull a prove it card. Prove it is true or false.

Card Letter	Prove That It's TRUE or FALSE
A	That 68 – 31 is the same as 67 – 30 because you can take 1 from both numbers and the difference is the same 68 – 31 = 37 and 67 – 30 = 37.

5,992 + 2,349 is the same as 6,000 + 2,341	2,125 + 1,151 is the same as 2,125 + 1,150 and 1 more
2,123 + 1,989 is the same as 2,000 and take 11 away	1,440 + 1,660 is the same as 1,450 + 1,650
68 – 31 is the same as 67 – 30	59 – 28 is the same as 60 – 30 and 1 more
99 – 45 is the same as 100 – 44 and take 2 away	31 – 15 is the same as 30 – 14

427 – 322 is the same as 425 – 320	543 – 127 is the same as 543 – 130 and 3 more
737 – 621 is the same as 740 – 621 and take 3 away	499 – 228 is the same as 500 – 229
2,095 – 1,050 is the same as 2,090 – 1,045	1,562 – 1,229 is the same as 1,562 – 1,230 and 1 more
8,183 – 7,040 is the same as 8,190 – 7,040 and take 7 away	9,099 – 2,073 is the same as 9,100 – 2,074

online resources ▸ Center cards and this recording sheet can be downloaded at **resources.corwin.com/FOF/ addsubtractwholenumber**.

ACTIVITY 4.16

Name: One and the Other   **Typr:** Center

About the Center: There are different ways to adjust numbers in order to use the Compensation strategy. Students need to practice different ways and develop proficiency, confidence, and preference of when and which approach to use if they adjust.

Materials: addition or subtraction expression cards, One and the Other recording sheet

Directions: 1. Students select an addition or subtraction problem.

2. Students solve the problem by adjusting one of the numbers in the problem.

3. Students solve the problem by adjusting both numbers in the problem.

4. Students star or signal the approach that they prefer for the problem.

TEACHING TAKEAWAY

Instead of making cards, you could provide a list of problems for students to choose from.

For example, a student selects 724 – 515. She adjusts one number by giving 1 to 724, making 725 – 515 = 210. Then, she takes the 1 away from 210 to equal 209. She then shows how she can adjust both numbers by taking 15 from both numbers and creating a problem, 709 – 500, with the same difference. She then stars the first option because she thinks it's easier to think about. Note that students don't have to write complete sentences to explain their thinking. You can even encourage them to use numbers and equations to show their thinking. Most any problem will work for the center. You can modify it for two-, four-, or five-digit numbers.

RESOURCE(S) FOR THIS ACTIVITY

	One and the Other	
Directions: Put an addition card. Show how you can solve it by adjusting one addend. Then show how you can solve it adjusting both addends. Put a star on the way you think is better		
Addition Problem	**Adjust one addend**	**Adjust both addends**
394 + 628	I can think 394 + 630 is 974. Then, take 2 away from 974 because I added too much. ☆	I can add 350 + 630 so give 950, when subtract 8 so equals 972.

	One and the Other	
Directions: Put a subtraction card. Show how you can solve it by adjusting one number. Then show how you can solve it by adjusting both numbers. Put a star on the way you think is better.		
Addition Problem	**Adjust One Addend**	**Adjust Both Addends**
709 – 515	I can give 1 to 724. I can think 725 – 515 = 210. Then, I can take 1 back. 210 – 1 = 209. ☆	I can take 15 from both numbers. 709 – 500 is 209. The difference is 209 because I took the same amount from both.

online resources ↘ These resources can be downloaded at **resources.corwin.com/FOF/addsubtractwholenumber**.

Think Addition Strategy

STRATEGY OVERVIEW:
Think Addition

What is Think Addition? This strategy is used for subtraction and uses the inverse relationship. Students rethink the subtraction expression as a missing addend equation and then solve it, which may also lead to using other strategies. For basic facts, the idea is that 15 – 7 is translated to mean 7 + ? = 15 (verbally, "How much more to get from my addend to my answer?"). A person either remembers their basic fact 7 + 8 = 15 (and therefore knows that 15 – 7 is 8) or uses reasoning, for example, knowing that 7 + 7 equals 14 and 1 more is 15, so the answer is 8. The same idea applies to multidigit numbers: a subtraction expression is translated, mentally or in writing, to an addition equation. 56 – 39 = ? For example, think 39 + ? = 56.

HOW DOES THINK ADDITION WORK?

Solving involves finding the difference between the two values (the missing addend). This can be done by **Counting Up**. Here are two different ways to count up:

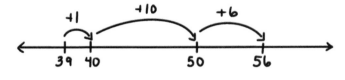

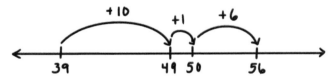

Counting Back is another option. Here is one of several ways:

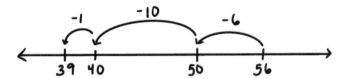

WHEN DO YOU CHOOSE THINK ADDITION?

This strategy is particularly useful when the two numbers being subtracted are close together (e.g., 472 – 458) or when both are near a benchmark (e.g., for 802 – 289, both are near a hundreds). Conversely, Think Addition is often not an efficient option when the minuend and subtrahend are far apart (e.g., 936 – 157).

THINK ADDITION:
Strategy Briefs for Families

It is important that families understand the strategies and know how they work so that they can be partners in the pursuit of fluency. These strategy briefs are a tool for doing that. You can include them in parent or school newsletters or share them at parent conferences. They are available for download so that you can adjust them as needed.

Think Addition Strategy for Subtraction

How It Works: We can use the relationship between addition and subtraction to solve subtraction problems. Subtraction is also a missing part addition problem.

1. Rethink the subtraction problem as a missing part addition problem.
2. Add up to find the missing part.
3. The missing part is the answer to the subtraction problem.

For example, 56 − 39 can be thought of as 39 plus something is 56. We can count up from 39 to 56, which is 17. So, 56 − 39 = 17.

When It's Useful: This strategy is useful when numbers are close together or when the Count Up or Count Back strategy isn't extensive.

Think Addition Strategy for Subtraction

How It Works: We can use the relationship between addition and subtraction to solve subtraction problems. Subtraction is also a missing part addition problem.

1. Rethink the subtraction problem as a missing part addition problem.
2. Add up to find the missing part.
3. The missing part is the answer to the subtraction problem.

For example, 802 − 289 can be thought of as 289 plus something is 802. We can count up from 289 to 802, which is 513. So, 802 − 289 = 513.

When It's Useful: This strategy is useful when numbers are close together or when the Count Up or Count Back strategy isn't extensive.

online resources → These resources can be downloaded at **resources.corwin.com/FOF/ addsubtractwholenumber**.

NOTES

_____

_____

_____

_____

MODULE 1 — Count On/ Count Back
MODULE 2 — Make Tens Strategy
MODULE 3 — Partial Sums and Differences Strategy
MODULE 4 — Compensation Strategy
MODULE 5 — Think Addition Strategy
MODULE 6 — Standard Algorithms for Addition and Subtraction

TEACHING ACTIVITIES for Think Addition

Before students are able to choose strategies, which is a key to fluency, they first must be able to understand and use relevant strategies. These activities focus specifically on Think Addition. While students may employ other methods to subtract, which is appropriate, they also must learn this important strategy that employs and strengthens their understanding of the relationship between addition and subtraction.

ACTIVITY 5.1
START WITH, GET TO (WITH HUNDRED CHARTS)

Students first learn about the inverse relationship between addition and subtraction in primary grades working with single-digit numbers. Students who show understanding of the concept with single-digit numbers may be challenged to transfer the understanding to two- and three-digit numbers. In this instructional activity, students advance their understanding of Think Addition by employing an idea of "start with, get to." First, students are shown a subtraction problem like 84 – 39. Then, students identify the potential Think Addition equation (39 + ? = 84). Students use this equation to establish the idea of "starting with one" number and counting on to "get to" the other. The Hundred Chart can be leveraged to support their thinking as needed.

91	92	93	94	95	96	97	98	99	100
			84	85	86	87	88	89	90
71	72	73	74	75	76	77	78	79	
61	62	63	64	65	66	67	68		70
51	52	53	54	55	56	57	58		60
41	42	43	44	45	46	47	48		50
31	32	33	34	35	36	37	38	39	40
21	22	23	24	25	26	27	28	29	30
11	12	13	14	15	16	17	18	19	20
1	2	3	4	5	6	7	8	9	10

$$84 - 39$$

$$\begin{array}{c} \text{start} \\ \text{with} \end{array} \qquad \begin{array}{c} \text{Get} \\ \text{to} \end{array}$$

$$39 + ? = 84$$
$$39 + 40 = 79$$
$$79 + 1 = 80$$
$$80 + 4 = 84$$

$$39 + 45 = 84 \text{ so}$$
$$84 - 39 = 45$$

As you facilitate the discussion, be sure to emphasize why one number is the "start with" and the other is the "get to." Keep in mind that these designations are opposite of counting back, so some students may be challenged to explain or represent their thinking.

TEACHING TAKEAWAY

You can provide base-10 blocks or place value disks to support students as they count up if needed.

RESOURCE(S) FOR THIS ACTIVITY

84 – 58	339 – 284	4,400 – 256	3,700 – 3,137
55 – 36	245 – 197	2,700 – 671	2,230 – 1,860
73 – 49	525 – 248	3,500 – 149	4,440 – 2,980
61 – 48	423 – 316	7,600 – 390	6,600 – 5,599
56 – 39	802 – 289	8,300 – 279	7,400 – 3,198

online resources These resources can be downloaded at **resources.corwin.com/FOF/addsubtractwholenumber**.

ACTIVITY 5.2
THINK ADDITION WITH BAR DIAGRAMS

Bar diagrams are excellent models for helping students develop understanding of the Think Addition relationship. For this activity, pose a subtraction expression to students such as 417 – 289. Have students work to create a bar diagram to represent the expression as an unknown difference using a bar diagram (left column in the following example). Then, have students determine the related Think Addition equation and count on to solve it (right column in the following example).

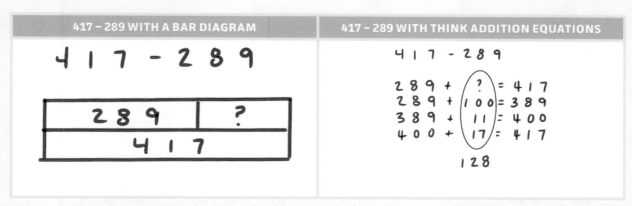

417 – 289 WITH A BAR DIAGRAM	417 – 289 WITH THINK ADDITION EQUATIONS

The bar diagram representations do not have to be proportionate to the numbers they represent. However, you could encourage students to think about half and determine which number is more than half. For example, in the bar diagram, the student determined that 289 is more than half of 417 and that the unknown is less than half of 417.

ACTIVITY 5.3
NUMBER LINE PROOFS

As students progress to subtracting four- and five-digit numbers, number charts and even bar diagrams can lose practicality. Number lines are good tools for representing this work. In this activity, students use number lines to prove that counting back in chunks to solve a subtraction problem yields the same solution as Think Addition. For example, a student was working to solve 4,456 – 2,380. In the following example on the left, the student shows how he jumped back to find a difference of 2,076. In the example on the right, he writes a Think Addition equation and then counts up to find the missing addend. His work shows that the sum of the jumps is 2,076, matching the difference from the first example.

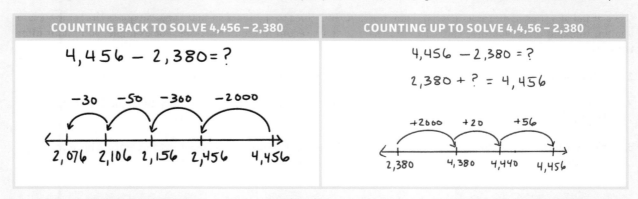

COUNTING BACK TO SOLVE 4,456 – 2,380	COUNTING UP TO SOLVE 4,4,56 – 2,380

These number line proofs work with any set of numbers. Teachers developing the strategy with two-digit numbers might be wise to make connections between this activity with the Hundred Chart and base-10 models. In all cases, it can be advantageous for students to have access to calculators to assure accuracy.

ACTIVITY 5.4
WHAT'S MISSING?

The triangle cards used in this activity vary slightly from the triangle fact cards students are familiar with, in that one of the numbers on the card is unknown. In this activity, students determine the missing value on a triangle card using addition and subtraction. Students should justify their thinking with pictures and numbers. After finding solutions, students should discuss how they found their solutions and should share the resulting addition and subtraction equations that the cards represent. During this discussion, you want to reinforce that addition can be a handy tool for finding differences.

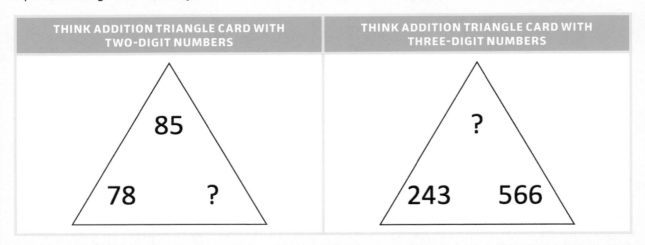

THINK ADDITION TRIANGLE CARD WITH TWO-DIGIT NUMBERS	THINK ADDITION TRIANGLE CARD WITH THREE-DIGIT NUMBERS
85 78 ?	? 243 566

Note that there are two different possibilities for the unknown number. With each card, students can find the sum or the difference of the two numbers presented. To compensate for this, you can circle one number (85 and 566, respectively) as the greatest number on each card. This will then create an addend unknown situation.

Also note that both of these cards are related to the Make Tens and Make Hundreds strategy. Be sure to focus students' attention during the discussion about how they used particular addition strategies to find sums for Think Addition situations.

ACTIVITY 5.5
WHAT'S THE TEMPERATURE?

Use a visual of a thermometer as a vertical number line. Give clues to students so that they can guess the temperature you are thinking of. As you give clues, be sure that students record related equations. For example, you might offer these clues:

1. In the morning it was 19 degrees. It warmed up 20 degrees. What's the temperature? (19 + 20 = 39)

2. When you got to school it was 67 degrees, but at recess time it was 52 degrees. How much did the temperature drop? (67 – 52 = 15)

3. It is 19 degrees. It has to be 32 degrees to go outside for recess. How much does the temperature have to go up? (32 – 19 = 13)

ACTIVITY 5.6
PROMPTS FOR TEACHING THINK ADDITION

Use the following prompts as opportunities to develop understanding of and reasoning with the strategy. Have students use representations and tools to justify their thinking, including base-10 models, number lines, number charts, and so on. After students work with the prompt(s), bring the class together to exchange ideas. These could be useful for collecting evidence of student understanding. Any prompt can be easily modified to feature different numbers (e.g., three-digit or four-digit numbers) and any prompt can be offered more than once if modified.

- Tell how you can use addition to solve a subtraction problem. Use examples to show your thinking.

- Jeremy says that 614 – 371 can be solved by thinking 371 + 614. Do you agree or disagree with Jeremy? Explain your thinking.

- Use a number line to show how 310 – 255 = ? is related to 255 + ? = 310.

- Stella uses Think Addition to solve 91 – 40. Tell why you agree or disagree with her thinking.

- Do you think that Think Addition will work with subtraction problems that subtract three-digit numbers from four-digit numbers? Prove your thinking with pictures or numbers.

- Tell how counting back and counting up (for Think Addition) are the same and how they are different.

- Jake used Think Addition to solve a subtraction problem. He added 300, then 40, then 7. What subtraction problem might he have solved?

- How would you explain Think Addition to someone new to your math class? Use examples to explain your thinking.

- Dak counts back to solve 1,460 – 354, taking away 354. Oscar counts up, using Think Addition. Which method makes the most sense for this problem?

- Lexa counted up to solve a subtraction problem. She counted up a total of 152. What might be the subtraction problem that Lexa solved.

- Do you prefer counting back or counting up to solve subtraction problems? Tell how they are the same and different. Use a problem like 554 – 126 to show your thinking.

- Jocelyn worked on the expression 2,300 – 1,871. Would it be more efficient for Jocelyn to count up or count back? Explain your answer.

NOTES

_____

_____

_____

_____

_____

PRACTICE ACTIVITIES for Think Addition

Fluency is realized through quality practice that is focused, varied, processed, and connected. The activities in this section focus students' attention on how this strategy works and when to use it. The activities are a collection of varied engagements. The discussion you facilitate after an activity or the reflection prompts you attach to it should help students think about what they did mathematically, how they reasoned about the activity, and when the math they did (namely the strategy) might be useful. Debriefing should also help students see how the practice activity connects to recent instruction or how the strategy connects to other strategies they know. Game boards, recording sheets, digit cards, and other required materials are available as online resources for you to download, possibly modify, and use. As students work with activities, you want to look for how well they are acquiring the strategy and assimilating it into their collection of strategies.

FLUENCY COMPONENT	WHAT TO LOOK FOR AS STUDENTS PRACTICE THIS STRATEGY
Efficiency	• Are students using the Think Addition strategy or are they reverting to previously learned and/or possibly less appropriate strategies? • Are students using the Think Addition strategy efficiently? (e.g., Do they count up in chunks or singles? Even when counting in chunks, do they count by tens or groups of 10?)
Flexibility	• Are students carrying out Think Addition in flexible ways? (e.g., Do they count up in different ways or do they count up in the same way each time?) • Do they change their approach to or from Think Addition as it proves inappropriate or overly complicated for the problem? (e.g., Do they begin to use partial differences for 317 – 298 and then switch to counting up?)
Accuracy	• Are students using the Think Addition strategy accurately? • Are students finding accurate solutions? • Are they considering the reasonableness of their solutions?* • Are students estimating before finding solutions?*

*This consideration is not unique to this strategy and should be practiced throughout the pursuit of fluency with whole numbers.

WORKED EXAMPLES

Worked examples are problems that have been solved. Correctly worked examples can help students make sense of a strategy and incorrectly worked examples attend to common errors.

Worked examples are excellent tools for this strategy, as students can compare examples to determine if they are better off thinking of the problem as take away or thinking of the problem as compare. Incorrectly worked examples can focus on the common counting errors students may have.

1. The student counts up by tens but struggles with the counting.
   - 831 – 765: counts up 765, 775, 785, … to get 825, and counts the distance as 70.
2. The student makes an error combining the parts in counting up or back.
   - 84 – 56: counts up 4 to 60, 20 to 80, and 4 to 84, but mis-adds or forgets a part.

Students may continue to count by single ones or tens or by hundreds instead of counting up in chunks. Worked examples can help students see flexible and efficient ways to use Think Addition. The prompts from Activity 5.6 can be used for collecting examples. Throughout the module are various worked examples that you can use as fictional worked examples. Additional ideas are provided in the following table.

SAMPLE WORKED EXAMPLES FOR THINK ADDITION

Correctly Worked Example

(make sense of the strategy)

What did _____ do?

Why does it work?

Is this a good method for this problem?

345 − 287 = ?

Compare these two ways to use Count Up:

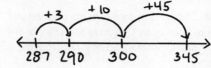

$$3 + 10 + 45 = 58$$

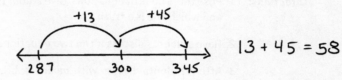

$$13 + 45 = 58$$

Partially Worked Example

(implement the strategy accurately)

Why did _____ start the problem this way?

What does _____ need to do to finish the problem?

Malinda's start:

7,418 − 5,750

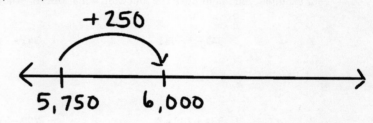

Incorrectly Worked Example

(highlight common errors)

What did _____ do?

What mistake does _____ make?

How can this mistake be fixed?

Nicholas' work:

409 − 187

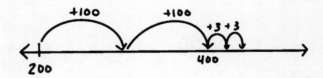

ACTIVITY 5.7

Name: "Two Lies and a Truth"   **Type:** Routine

About the Routine: Students may seem to understand Think Addition situations by connecting addition and subtraction equations. However, they may not truly or fully understand the relationship and how to use it because they instead rely on gross generalizations. This routine aims to develop a deeper, accurate understanding of the Think Addition strategy.

Materials: This routine does not require any materials.

Directions: 1. Pose three pairs of equations. Give students individual think time to decide which two pairs are lies, and which one is a truth.

2. Have students discuss if the two equations are related through the Think Addition strategy.

3. After students discuss with partners, bring the group together to share ideas. When students identify equations that aren't related, have them determine a new equation that would be related to one of the equations.

For example, you might pose the following equations for students to discuss.

1	$341 - ? = 561$	$341 + ? = 561$	Students might believe these are related through Think Addition because both equations have the same numbers and are in the same order.
2	$334 + 789 = ?$	$789 - 334 = ?$	Similar to the first example, these equations have the same number. Also note that the subtraction equation has a larger minuend, which some students may rely on for determining correct subtraction expressions.
3	$664 - ? = 455$	$455 + ? = 664$	This is a correct Think Addition.

ACTIVITY 5.8

Name: "Jump in Chunks"   **Type:** Routine

About the Routine: Estimating differences supports reasonableness. Estimating the size of chunks to count up is also a very useful skill for being efficient. An example is 4,456 – 2,380, shown in Activity 5.2. When using Think Addition, a student can jump 2,000 forward from 2,380 to 4,380. But a jump of 100 more (4,380 to 4,480) will be too much. In this routine, students practice making jumps that are close but not too much.

Materials: This routine does not require any materials.

Directions:

1. Pose a subtraction problem recorded on the board.

2. Students determine what the related Think Addition equation would be and share that. Record this equation on the board.

3. Ask students to think about the first chunk that they would add. Remind students that they should try to use the most efficient jump that they can add easily.

4. Students share their thinking with a partner and then you have a brief discussion, accepting all ideas but settling on one option.

5. Record the jump using a number line and/or equation and ask students to think of the chunk they would add next.

For example, 716 – 488 is posed to students who rethink the problem as a Think Addition problem and share it. The teacher records it as 488 + ? = 716 and asks students to think about the jumps that they would make to get close to 716. A student shares that their first jump would be +200 to get to 688. The student also shares that a jump of 300 would be too much (788 is more than 716). Another student shares their first jump to be 120 because 488 and a jump of 220 is easy to think about arriving at 608. The class briefly debates which jump is easiest and the teacher records the thinking. Now at 608, the teacher asks what the next jump would be. A student shares that 100 would get them to 708. Others agree and the teacher records the additional jump, stopping at 708. Students then think about the next jump. Some think there are two jumps (one to 710 and one to 716). Others quickly see a related basic fact and argue for a final jump of 8.

ACTIVITY 5.9

Name: The Smallest Difference   **Type:** Game

About the Game: Reasoning about results supports the accuracy component of fluency. *The Smallest Difference* helps students practice reasoning by having them determine what numbers will generate the smallest difference. You can enrich the experience by having students estimate differences before finding exact solutions.

Materials: prepared deck of 12 or more multidigit number cards

Directions:
1. The deck of number cards is shuffled and players are dealt three cards.

2. Players choose two of the three cards to make a subtraction problem.

3. Players use Think Addition to find the difference of the two cards they kept.

4. The player with the smallest difference gets a point.

5. All cards are returned to the deck, the deck is shuffled, and players are dealt three cards again.

6. Play continues until a player earns 5 points.

Any numbers can be used for this game. Cards can be easily made with index cards or number cards can be printed on cardstock. Examples of a set of cards for two-digit and three-digit play are as follows:

RESOURCE(S) FOR THIS ACTIVITY

975	452	463	881
478	791	184	540
328	176	441	744
519	667	772	315
390	536	519	128

97	45	63	81
78	91	84	54
28	17	44	74
19	66	77	31
90	36	19	28

 These resources can be downloaded at **resources.corwin.com/FOF/addsubtractwholenumber**.

ACTIVITY 5.10

Name: Target 0 or Bust   **Type:** Game

About the Game: Like other target games, *Target 0 or Bust* is a game for practicing subtraction and developing estimation sense and reasoning.

Materials: two sets of digit cards (0–9) or playing cards (queens = 0, aces = 1, kings and jacks removed) per player, *Target 0 or Bust* recording sheet

Directions: 1. Each player begins with 1,000 points with the goal of having the most points when any opponent hits zero.

2. Digit cards are shuffled and six cards are dealt so that each player can make 2 three-digit numbers.

3. Each player arranges their digits to create 2 three-digit numbers that have a difference as close to zero as possible.

4. After arranging the digits, the players find the difference using Think Addition.

5. The difference of the two numbers is subtracted from the players' 1,000 points.

6. Players then reshuffle and play round 2. After finding the difference, the players subtract that amount from their remaining balance of points.

7. The person with the highest balance after 6 rounds wins.

The following table shows Taylor's first three rounds of the game. After three rounds, she has a balance of 753 points.

ROUND	DIGITS PULLED	SMALLEST DIFFERENCE	POINT BALANCE
Round 1	5, 6, 7, 3, 3, and 4	364 − 357 = 7	993 (1,000 − 7)
Round 2	1, 4, 3, 9, 4, and 7	913 − 714 = 169	824 (993 − 169)
Round 3	2, 2, 8, 3, 9, and 5	922 − 853 = 69	755 (824 − 69)

RESOURCE(S) FOR THIS ACTIVITY

Target 0 or Bust

Directions: Deal yourself six digit cards. Create a subtraction problem with the smallest difference. Rethink the subtraction problem as a Think Addition equation. Find the difference. Subtract the difference from your point balance.

Round	Digits	Subtraction Problem	Think Addition Equation	Difference	Point Balance Start With 1,000

 Digit cards and this recording sheet can be downloaded at **resources.corwin.com/FOF/ addsubtractwholenumber**.

ACTIVITY 5.11

Name: Think Addition Math Libs   **Type:** Game

About the Game: Games do not always have to be ripe with strategy. Rather simplistic games of chance can be enjoyed by students. *Think Addition Math Libs* is a race to complete the equations.

Materials: *Think Addition Math Libs* game board; digit cards (0–9), playing cards (queens = 0, aces = 1, kings and jacks removed), or spinner

Directions: 1. Players take turns pulling a digit card and using the number to fill a space on their board.

2. Once a player fully completes a problem, they use Think Addition to find the unknown. Their opponent also finds the unknown to confirm they are correct (but cannot record it on their game board).

3. A player loses their turn if a digit they pull can't be used for any space on their board.

4. The first player to find all of the unknowns correctly wins.

For example, on Jackson's first turn he pulled a 9. He used it to complete 790 + ? = 1,145 and then he found the unknown. His partner took a turn and on Jackson's next turn he pulled a 3, completing the top row.

Think Addition Math Libs

Directions: Take turns choosing a digit card. Use the digit to fill in a number in the Think Addition column. Once a number is completely filled, find the value for the question mark (?). Be the first to find all of the question marks.

556 – 334 = ?	3 _3_ 4 + ? = 556	? = 222
619 – 277 = ?	277 + ? = 61__	? =
981 – 317 = ?	__17 + ? = 981	? =
1,145 – 790 = ?	7 _9_ 0 + ? = 1,145	? = 355

online resources This resource can be downloaded at **resources.corwin.com/FOF/addsubtractwholenumber**.

ACTIVITY 5.12

Name: Think Addition Blocks   **Type:** Center

About the Center: Place value models help students represent and make sense of Think Addition.

Materials: digit cards (0–9) or playing cards (queens = 0, aces = 1, kings and jacks removed), Think Addition Blocks recording sheet

Directions: 1. Students choose four cards and create two-digit numbers.

2. Students create a subtraction expression and write it on their recording sheet.

3. Students create a related Think Addition expression.

4. To figure out the missing addend, students draw base-10 sticks and dots to help them add up to the sum.

5. Students then write the subtraction equation.

For example, a student pulls four digit cards and creates the expression 56 – 39. The student would write the expression on the recording sheet. The student then creates the inverse expression. In this example, it would be 39 + ? = 56. At this point the student draws base-10 blocks to find the missing addend. The student draws a base-10 stick and seven dots to represent 17. Once the missing addend is found, the student can go back to the original expression and write the difference 56 – 39 = 17.

RESOURCE(S) FOR THIS ACTIVITY

Think Addition Blocks

Directions: Take four cards to create 2 two-digit numbers. Write a subtraction problem. Write a related Think Addition problem. Draw base-10 blocks to help you count up to the sum.

Subtraction Problem	Think Addition Problem	Base-10 Drawing
56 – 39 =	39 + ___ = 56	39 + ┃ ⫶⫶

1	2	3	4
5	6	7	8
9	1	2	3
4	5	6	7
8	9	0	0

online resources ↘ This resource can be downloaded at **resources.corwin.com/FOF/addsubtractwholenumber**.

ACTIVITY 5.13

Name: Triangle Cards   **Type:** Center

About the Center: Triangle fact cards help students develop addition and subtraction basic fact recall. These cards focus students on the relationship between the three numbers through either of the operations. This center builds on that by using larger numbers. Any activity that makes use of a basic fact triangle card could be modified for use with these cards.

Materials: triangle cards, recording sheet

Directions:
1. Students select a triangle card.

2. The student writes the two addition equations the card represents and the two subtraction equations the card represents.

3. For example, a student picks the card on the left. They record 815 + 95 = 910, 95 + 815 = 910, 910 – 95 = 815, and 910 – 815 = 95.

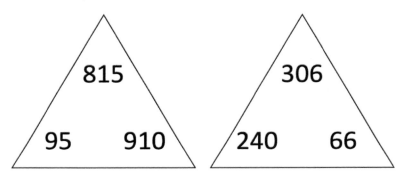

A modified version of this center presents two of the three numbers within the equation as shown in Activity 5.4 ("What's Missing?"). Students then determine what the missing number is and record all of the equations.

RESOURCE(S) FOR THIS ACTIVITY

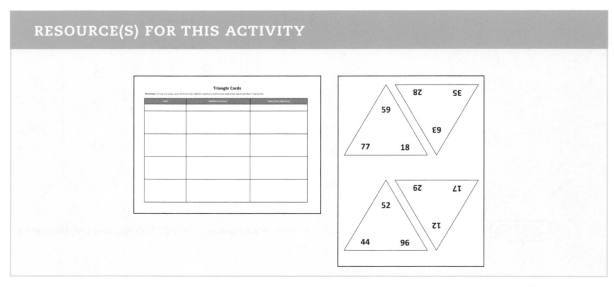

Triangle cards and this recording sheet can be downloaded at **resources.corwin.com/FOF/addsubtractwholenumber**.

ACTIVITY 5.14

Name: Guess and Check   **Type:** Center

About the Center: Estimating sums and differences supports determining reasonableness. This center provides an opportunity to estimate a difference and then check it with calculations and a calculator.

Materials: subtraction cards, Guess and Check recording sheet, calculator

Directions:

1. Students select a subtraction card.

2. They estimate the difference.

3. Then students write the related Think Addition equation and add up to solve the problem.

4. Students check their accuracy with a calculator and determine if their estimate was reasonable.

> **TEACHING TAKEAWAY**
>
> It is a good idea to provide students with a calculator to support their accuracy. Using a calculator also provides an extra dose of practice.

RESOURCE(S) FOR THIS ACTIVITY

Guess and Check With Think Addition

Directions: Pick a subtraction card. Estimate the difference. Rewrite the problem as Think Addition. Add up to find the difference and check your work with a calculator.

Write the Subtraction Problem	Estimate the Difference	Write the Problem as a Think Addition Problem	Add Up to Show the Solution Check Your Work With a Calculator

online resources — This resource can be downloaded at **resources.corwin.com/FOF/addsubtractwholenumber**.

ACTIVITY 5.15

Name: *Sentence Strip Reverso*   **Type:** *Center*

About the Center: This center is an opportunity to practice connecting subtraction equations with unknown addend equations. After creating the relationship, students add up to find a solution.

Materials: sentence strips with subtraction or unknown addend equations, recording sheet

Directions:
1. Students choose a sentence strip.

2. Students record the equation from the sentence strip in the corresponding column of the recording sheet.

3. Students then record the related subtraction or Think Addition equation.

4. Students then add up to find the unknown and show their thinking on the recording sheet.

Any collection of subtraction problems or unknown addend problems can be used with this center. Possibilities include the following:

TEACHING TAKEAWAY

Classroom volunteers can make sentence strips for this center. Provide them with a list of equations you want them to use.

RESOURCE(S) FOR THIS ACTIVITY

$48 + ? = 65$	$448 + ? = 665$
$34 + ? = 63$	$314 + ? = 363$
$45 + ? = 82$	$435 + ? = 682$
$77 + ? = 101$	$177 + ? = 801$
$88 + ? = 114$	$488 + ? = 514$

$4,802 + ? = 2,657$	$28 + ? = 91$
$3,244 + ? = 1,630$	$728 + ? = 791$
$4,548 + ? = 2,825$	$2,849 + ? = 191$
$7,712 + ? = 1,018$	$95 + ? = 910$
$8,383 + ? = 4,114$	$66 + ? = 306$

$2,393 - 1,740 = ?$	$32 - 18 = ?$
$5,367 - 3,816 = ?$	$320 - 183 = ?$
$1,817 - 1,048 = ?$	$3,255 - 1,892 = ?$
$7,179 - 5,900 = ?$	$910 - 815 = ?$
$4,920 - 2,514 = ?$	$306 - 240 = ?$

Sentence Strip Reverso

Directions: Select a sentence strip. Write the problem on the recording sheet. Write the related problem. Add up to find the solution.

Subtraction Problem	Think Addition (Add Until Even)	Solution

online resources — Center cards and this recording sheet can be downloaded at **resources.corwin.com/FOF/ addsubtractwholenumber**.

ACTIVITY 5.16

Name: Make the Difference   **Type:** Center

About the Center: This center challenges students to create different problems that have the same difference. It intends to practice Think Addition and problem solving.

Materials: digit cards (0–9) or playing cards (queens = 0, aces = 1, kings and jacks removed), recording sheet

Directions:
1. Students select digit cards to make a number. To note, the number of cards can be adjusted for use with any problem.

2. Students create two different problems that have a difference equal to the number they made with the digit cards.

3. Students rewrite using Think Addition to justify the problems they created.

For example, Mel pulled three-digit cards 3, 4, and 1, making 341. She created 741 – 400 and 651 – 310. She used Think Addition to prove that the difference of each was 341.

Notes about Make the Difference: At first, you may choose to let students come up with anything they like. However, you might find patterns in their thinking. For example, Mel's first problem (741 – 400) is pretty easy to deduce. You may find that students begin to create lots of problems like this (e.g., 841 – 500, 941 – 600, or 641 – 300). If this happens, you can begin to put restrictions on the type of numbers they have to use. For example, you might say neither number can have a zero.

Two-digit differences can be found between three-digit numbers, four-digit numbers, and so on. You might consider giving an explicit size for the minuend and subtrahend.

RESOURCE(S) FOR THIS ACTIVITY

Make the Difference		

1	2	3	4
5	6	7	8
9	1	2	3
4	5	6	7
8	9	0	0

online resources ↘ Digit cards and this recording sheet can be downloaded at **resources.corwin.com/FOF/ addsubtractwholenumber**.

Standard Algorithms for Addition and Subtraction

STRATEGY OVERVIEW:
Standard Algorithms

What is a Standard Algorithm? Algorithms vary from country to country, and even region to region. In the United States, standard algorithms for multidigit addition and subtraction involve using Partial Sums or Differences, beginning with the ones place and working to the left (larger) place values. While some believe that using tick marks is part of the standard algorithm, notations do not define an algorithm (Fuson & Beckmann, 2012–2013). All three of the following examples, in fact, use the U.S. standard algorithm for addition:

TICK MARKS NOTATED ABOVE	TICK MARKS NOTATED BELOW	NO TICK MARKS, PARTIALS RECORDED
635 + 378 = 1,013	635 + 378 = 1,013	635 + 378; 13; 100; 900; 1,013

HOW DO U.S. STANDARD ALGORITHMS WORK?

Standard algorithms are truly a place value strategy. For addition, the idea is that when there are more than 10 in any place, they are regrouped to the next higher place value. Subtraction utilizes decomposing. When subtraction would result in a negative value, the place value to the left is decomposed, moving a group of 10 to the right, in order to get a whole number difference.

WHEN DO YOU CHOOSE A STANDARD ALGORITHM?

While standard algorithms always work, they are not always the best choice. A standard algorithm is needed in the following situations:

• Numbers in the problem do not lend themselves to a mental method.

• Numbers in the problem do not lend themselves to a convenient written option (e.g., compensation).

• You don't know an alternate method.

• You want to check an answer having used a different method.

Perhaps because standard algorithms are in state standards, a major part of our own learning, and applicable to all problems, there can be a hurry to get to them and significantly more time devoted to learning them than their reasoning alternatives. This is a mistake. A rush to the standard algorithm and memorizing procedures undermines students' confidence and may cause math anxiety, negatively impacting achievement (Boaler, 2015a, b; Jameson, 2013; Ramirez, Shaw, & Maloney, 2018). Note that "fluently add" does not mean "use the standard algorithm adeptly." It means you use the standard algorithm adeptly *when it is the most efficient option*. Such flexibility is at the heart of ensuring students develop fluency.

STANDARD ALGORITHMS:
Strategy Briefs for Families

It is important that families understand the strategies and know how they work so that they can be partners in the pursuit of fluency. These strategy briefs are a tool for doing that. You can include them in parent or school newsletters or share them at parent conferences. They are available for download so that you can adjust them as needed.

Standard Algorithm for Addition

How It Works: Addends are aligned vertically by place value. Each place value is added from right to left. When a sum is more than 10, it is regrouped. Regrouping can be recorded above the addends or below them.

In the examples, 5 + 8 = 13. Since 13 is more than 10, it needs to be regrouped. Record the 3 in the ones and regroup the 1 ten. That 1 ten added to 3 tens and 7 tens equals 11 tens or 1 hundred and 1 ten. Record the 1 ten and regroup the 1 hundred.

Things to Remember:

- Place values are being added. In 635 + 378, 3 tens are being added to 7 tens.

- Knowing when to use an algorithm is just as important as knowing how to use an algorithm. Problems like 200 + 300 do not need an algorithm for solving.

- Students should always think about what is a reasonable answer. In this problem, an answer around 1,000 would be reasonable because the problem can be thought of as 600 + 400. Students may also estimate 900 because the problem can be thought of as 600 + 300.

$$
\begin{array}{r} 635 \\ + 378 \\ \hline 1,013 \end{array}
\qquad
\begin{array}{r} 635 \\ + 378 \\ \hline 1,013 \end{array}
$$

Standard Algorithm for Subtraction

How It Works: Numbers are aligned vertically by place value. Each place value is subtracted from right to left. The right example, 819 – 476, requires regrouping, meaning 7 tens cannot be taken from 1 ten. If subtracted it would lead to a negative number. The 8 hundreds becomes 7 hundreds and 10 tens. Those 10 tens and 1 more ten make 11 tens. The 7 tens can be taken from 11 tens, leaving 4 tens as shown below.

Things to Remember:

- Place values are being subtracted. In the left example (684 – 231), 3 tens are subtracted from 8 tens and 2 hundreds are being subtracted from 6 hundreds.

- Knowing when to use an algorithm is just as important as knowing how to use an algorithm. A problem like 500 – 300 should not need an algorithm for solving.

- Students should always think about what is a reasonable answer. In the problem on the right, 400 is reasonable by thinking 800 – 400. 300 could also be reasonable by thinking 800 – 500. As you see, the actual difference is close to both 400 and 300.

$$
\begin{array}{r} 684 \\ - 231 \\ \hline 453 \end{array}
\qquad
\begin{array}{r} 819 \\ - 476 \\ \hline 343 \end{array}
$$

 These resources can be downloaded at **resources.corwin.com/FOF/ addsubtractwholenumber**.

NOTES

_____

_____

_____

_____

_____

MODULE 1 Count On/ Count Back

MODULE 2 Make Tens Strategy

MODULE 3 Partial Sums and Differences Strategy

MODULE 4 Compensation Strategy

MODULE 5 Think Addition Strategy

MODULE 6 Standard Algorithms for Addition and Subtraction

TEACHING ACTIVITIES for
Standard Algorithms

Explicit strategy instruction for standard algorithms has been a pillar of elementary school. The use of base-10 blocks and other tools has helped students to conceptually see the regrouping. Because standard algorithms are less intuitive and have numerous steps, it is even more important to focus on reasonableness. When the focus is on standard algorithms, students may see opportunities for reasoning strategies. Use these moments to address efficiency. For example, ask, "How does the [Make Hundred] strategy compare to the standard algorithm?" Engaging the class in such a discussion places fluency as the focus (not just mastering an algorithm).

ACTIVITY 6.1
THEY ARE THE SAME!

Standard algorithms for addition and subtraction are abstract procedures. Many students, even those with early success, can forget how to carry out the algorithm over time. However, proficiency and retention increase if students understand what is happening. Often this occurs by using base-10 models to demonstrate the carrying out of the algorithm. This activity functions differently and might be offered before the process is taught.

Provide students with a completed problem, a base-10 model representation, and a completed algorithm. Then ask students to identify what they observe and what they wonder about the three examples. After sharing, tell students that all three show the same thing and the sums are correct. Then ask students to find exactly how they are related.

PROBLEM	BASE-10 MODEL	ALGORITHM
1 3 4 + 2 5 5 = 389	□ ∥∣ ···· □ □ ∥∥∥∣ ·····	1 3 4 + 2 5 5 —— 3 8 9

For example, students might share that all three examples show one 100 in the first number or that each has the same number of hundreds, tens, and ones. You might repeat the activity before extending it. To do so, give students two of the three examples and have them work with partners to find the missing example. For example, to extend, a teacher gave the problem 614 + 252 = 866 and the algorithm. Students would then have to determine the base-10 model and tell how all three are connected.

PROBLEM	BASE-10 MODEL	ALGORITHM
6 1 4 + 2 5 2 = 866	□ □ □ ∣ ···· □ □ □ □ □ ∥∥∣ ·· ∣	6 1 4 + 2 5 2 —— 8 6 6

Early work should use situations that don't call for regrouping. You can shift to regrouping soon after students show understanding of non-regrouping situations.

PROBLEM	BASE-10 MODEL	ALGORITHM
263 + 418 = 681	□ □ |||| ·· || □ □ |||| :::: □ □	$\begin{array}{r} {}^{1}\\ 2\,6\,3 \\ +\,4\,1\,8 \\ \hline 6\,8\,1 \end{array}$

ACTIVITY 6.2
CONNECTING PARTIALS AND ALGORITHMS

In many cases, standards algorithms are streamlined versions of Partial Sums and Differences. You can leverage students' understanding of Partial Sums and Differences to make sense of the algorithms. To do this, provide a completed algorithm and ask students to find the Partial Sums or Differences. Once completed, discuss how the algorithm and the recording of partials is similar and different.

Look at the left column in the following example. Students should notice that the addends are the same and that there are similar digits in the sum. They should also notice that 700 + 40 + 9 is the same as the 749 shown in the standard algorithm. The right example has a similar feature. In it, the sum of the partials, 30 and 11, is clearly evident in the result of the standard algorithm.

PROBLEM: 514 + 235		PROBLEM: 623 + 418	
$\begin{array}{l} 500 + 200 = 700 \\ 10 + 30 = 40 \\ 4 + 5 = 9 \end{array}$	$\begin{array}{r} 514 \\ +235 \\ \hline 749 \end{array}$	$\begin{array}{l} 600 + 400 = 1{,}000 \\ 20 + 10 = 30 \\ 3 + 8 = 11 \end{array}$	$\begin{array}{r} {}^{1}\\ 623 \\ +418 \\ \hline 1{,}041 \end{array}$
$\begin{array}{r} 500 + 10 + 4 \\ +200 + 30 + 5 \\ \hline 700 + 40 + 9 \end{array}$	$\begin{array}{r} 514 \\ +235 \\ \hline 749 \end{array}$	$\begin{array}{r} 600 + 20 + 3 \\ +400 + 10 + 8 \\ \hline 1{,}000 + 30 + 11 \end{array}$	$\begin{array}{r} {}^{1}\\ 623 \\ +418 \\ \hline 1{,}041 \end{array}$

Of course, regrouping presents a different challenge. Even so, when a partial sums recording is situated close to an algorithm, students should be able to make connections between the recordings. You can extend the activity to provide algorithms and charge students with creating the partial sums recordings. Note that the examples only show addition but that a version for subtraction would function in the same way.

ACTIVITY 6.3
TO ALGORITHM OR NOT
TO ALGORITHM

Fluency with standard algorithms includes not only how to use an algorithm but *when* to use an algorithm. It is critical that we empower students to think critically about when they need this tool. This activity aims to do just that. Pose a collection of addition or subtraction problems to small groups of students. Have the students think about which problems call for an algorithm and which don't. Students must show their strategies for problems that don't call for an algorithm. Conversely, students must tell why a certain problem is best suited for the algorithm.

Use Algorithm	Don't Use Algorithm
267 + 377	318 + 400
719 + 455	899 + 236
916 + 248	625 + 125

In this example, the teacher posed a list of six different problems. Students worked with partners to sort and record those problems. They explained (*not shown*) that 318 + 400 was easy to count on by hundreds, that you could give 1 to 899 to make a 100, and that they could add 600 + 100 and 25 + 25 to solve the last problem. They determined that these three didn't require the use of an algorithm.

ACTIVITY 6.4
RETHINKING SUBTRACTION
WITH ZEROS

It can be challenging for students to acquire subtraction with one or more zeros using the standard algorithm. However, problems like 700 – 268 may not need to be the stressful hassle they have been traditionally. Instead, students can call on ideas of compensation to solve these problems. This activity revisits compensation and builds on the notion of constant difference presented in Activity 4.5 ("Meter Stick Compensation"). In fact, you might want to revisit that activity to initiate this one. After ensuring that students are comfortable adjusting both minuends and subtrahends, pose a problem like 700 – 268. Give students time to struggle using the algorithm to solve the problem. Then, discuss how you might adjust the problem. 700 – 268 is the same as 699 – 267 and no regrouping is necessary (see the left column in the following example).

$$
\begin{array}{c}
\overset{6\ 9\ 10}{7\cancel{0}\cancel{0}} \\
-\,2\,6\,8 \\
\hline
4\ 3\ 2
\end{array}
\qquad
\begin{array}{c}
6\,9\,9 \\
-\,2\,6\,7 \\
\hline
4\ 3\ 2
\end{array}
\qquad\qquad
\begin{array}{c}
\overset{5\ 9\ 11}{2,6\cancel{0}\cancel{1}} \\
-\,1,3\,8\,9 \\
\hline
1,2\,1\,2
\end{array}
\qquad
\begin{array}{c}
2,6\,1\,2 \\
-\,1,4\,0\,0 \\
\hline
1,2\,1\,2
\end{array}
$$

Help students determine if adjusting to use the standard algorithm always works by examining other problems like 511 – 478, in which you can take 12 from each. And there are other compensations to explore. For example, 2,601 – 1,389 might be easier to think about by adding 11 to both numbers, which creates 2,612 – 1,400 and doesn't need to be regrouped either (see the right example).

TEACHING TAKEAWAY

Two-digit problems, such as 90 – 38, can be investigated as well. However, we don't believe that these problems should ever be solved with an algorithm.

ACTIVITY 6.5
PROMPTS FOR TEACHING STANDARD ALGORITHMS

Use the following prompts as opportunities to develop understanding of and reasoning with the strategy. Have students use representations and tools to justify their thinking, including base-10 models, number lines, number charts, and so on. After students work with the prompt(s), bring the class together to exchange ideas. These could be useful for collecting evidence of student understanding. Any prompt can be easily modified to feature different numbers (e.g., three-digit or four-digit numbers) and any prompt can be offered more than once if modified.

- Tell how the addition/subtraction algorithm works. Use examples to explain your thinking.

- Maria solved 614 – 386. Her work follows. Do you agree with Maria's work? Why or why not?

$$
\begin{array}{c}
\overset{\ \ 10\ \ 13}{6\cancel{1}\cancel{4}} \\
-\,3\,8\,6 \\
\hline
3\ 2\ 7
\end{array}
$$

- Identify two addition/subtraction problems that you don't need an algorithm to solve. Tell why you don't need an algorithm for those two problems.

- Dennis estimated that 3,680 – 2,390 was about 4,000 to help him in case he made a mistake using the algorithm. Do you agree with his estimate?

(Continued)

(Continued)

- How does estimating a sum or difference help when you are using an algorithm?

- Connie changed 4,300 – 2,688 to 4,299 – 2,687. Can she do this? Do you think it will help her find the difference?

- Tina subtracts a three-digit number from a three-digit number and gets a correct answer of 548. What might the two numbers be?

- What is a number that when added to 743 would need an algorithm to solve?

- Natasha subtracted 400 – 246 by changing the expression to 399 – 246 and then added 1 more. Thomas said Natasha was incorrect because that would give her an incorrect difference. Is Thomas correct? Why or why not?

- Find and correct the error(s).

$$
\begin{array}{r}
\overset{2}{4}37 \\
+\ 135 \\
\hline
381
\end{array}
$$

NOTES

_____

_____

_____

_____

_____

_____

_____

_____

PRACTICE ACTIVITIES for Standard Algorithms

Fluency is realized through quality practice that is focused, varied, processed, and connected. The activities in this section focus students' attention on how this strategy works and when to use it. The activities are a collection of varied engagements. The discussion you facilitate after an activity or the reflection prompts you attach to it should help students think about what they did mathematically, how they reasoned about the activity, and when the math they did (namely the strategy) might be useful. Debriefing should also help students see how the practice activity connects to recent instruction or how the strategy connects to other strategies they know. Game boards, recording sheets, digit cards, and other required materials are available as online resources for you to download, possibly modify, and use. As students work with activities, you want to look for how well they are acquiring the strategy and assimilating it into their collection of strategies.

FLUENCY COMPONENT	WHAT TO LOOK FOR AS STUDENTS PRACTICE THE ALGORITHMS
Efficiency	• Are students using the algorithm when another strategy is clearly more useful? • Are students using the algorithm efficiently? • Do they use the algorithm regardless of its appropriateness for the problem at hand?
Flexibility	• Are students using the algorithm when it is unnecessary? (e.g., 600 – 300) • Do students change their approach to or from the algorithm as it proves inappropriate or overly complicated for the problem?
Accuracy	• Are students using the algorithm accurately? • Are students finding accurate solutions when using the algorithm? • Are they considering the reasonableness of their solutions?* • Are students estimating before they use the algorithm?

*This consideration is not unique to this strategy and should be practiced throughout the pursuit of fluency with whole numbers.

WORKED EXAMPLES

Worked examples are opportunities for students to analyze the thinking of another student. Worked examples include correct and incorrect examples. While algorithms always work, the enactment of established steps and notations can lead to mistakes along the way. Worked examples focused on common errors can help students develop an understanding of why that step does not work.

The prompts from Activity 6.5 can be used for collecting examples. Throughout the module are various examples that you can use as worked examples. The table here shows common errors and a sample worked example with that error. Because standard algorithms are error prone, estimating and checking for reasonableness are very important. When you analyze worked examples, you can begin by asking, "Is this answer reasonable?" If the answer is "no," then ask, "What is a reasonable answer?" Of course, there are wrong answers that turn out to be reasonable, which is why it is also good to check for accuracy, either by rechecking the steps or using the inverse operation with the answer.

COMMON ERROR	WORKED EXAMPLE
Adds partial sums but does not regroup them	$\begin{array}{r} 43 \\ +\ 59 \\ \hline 912 \end{array}$
Adds numbers from different place values, especially when number lengths vary	$\begin{array}{r} \overset{1}{3}24 \\ +\quad 58 \\ \hline 882 \end{array}$
Finds the differences, not attending to which quantity is being taken away from the other	$\begin{array}{r} 63 \\ -27 \\ \hline 44 \end{array}\qquad \begin{array}{r} 7\overset{0}{\cancel{1}}\overset{16}{\cancel{6}} \\ -137 \\ \hline 639 \end{array}$
Regroups incorrectly across zeros	$\begin{array}{r} \overset{3}{\cancel{4}}\overset{1}{0}\overset{1}{2} \\ -246 \\ \hline 166 \end{array}\qquad \begin{array}{r} \overset{4}{\cancel{5}}\overset{9}{\cancel{0}}\overset{9}{\cancel{0}}1 \\ -4,195 \\ \hline 806 \end{array}$

ACTIVITY 6.6

Name: "Between and About"　　　　**Type:** Routine

About the Routine: Students often make mistakes with algorithms and don't realize that their solution is unreasonable. Reasonableness plays a role in fluency. So, practicing it has significant implications, especially for determining accuracy when using algorithms. Additionally, determining reasonableness cannot become an additional procedure. There are a variety of ways to estimate; this routine offers practice in two of them.

Materials: This routine does not require any materials.

Directions: Post a series of expressions to students, one at a time. Have students determine the range for the answer as it is between _____ and _____. Record different ideas for the range and discuss as a class which ideas make the most sense. After a *between* number is agreed upon by the group, students then look to find an *about* number that is a reasonable estimate (using rounding, front-end estimation, or compatibles, as they like). Students should not be asked to find the exact answer. It can be revealed after the between number and the about number are identified.

PROBLEM POSED	BETWEEN	ABOUT
346 + 519	800 and 1,000 819 and 919	800, 900, 819, 846
732 + 848	1,500 and 1,600 1,548 and 1,648 1,532 and 1,632	1,500, 1,600, 1,532

In the example, some students found a range by using friendly numbers for both addends, whereas other students used a friendly number for just one addend. Estimates for these sums functioned in the same way by finding friendlies for both addends and only one addend in other cases. The routine works with any set of problems. Some to consider include the following:

ADDING TWO-DIGIT NUMBERS	ADDING THREE-DIGIT NUMBERS	ADDING FOUR-DIGIT NUMBERS	ADDING FIVE-DIGIT NUMBERS
32 + 59	553 + 797	9,699 + 5,978	43,201 + 72,909
16 + 54	279 + 619	1,023 + 9,807	37,835 + 12,451
37 + 49	605 + 327	4,178 + 1,247	67,489 + 23,632
46 + 25	428 + 565	1,653 + 7,803	58,588 + 27,375
56 + 16	105 + 199	3,915 + 2,091	79,035 + 10,384
SUBTRACTING TWO-DIGIT NUMBERS	**SUBTRACTING THREE-DIGIT NUMBERS**	**SUBTRACTING FOUR-DIGIT NUMBERS**	**SUBTRACTING FIVE-DIGIT NUMBERS**
45 – 26	452 – 237	2,792 – 1,744	95,275 – 23,461
61 – 33	642 – 226	3,562 – 2,108	69,366 – 16,725
74 – 58	728 – 137	5,205 – 3,565	89,156 – 58,429
95 – 17	554 – 226	4,374 – 3,802	50,648 – 37,142
86 – 48	659 – 287	9,003 – 6,530	57,599 – 36,179

ACTIVITY 6.7

Name: "That One" **Type:** Routine

About the Routine: This routine helps students consider when to use an algorithm. It is intended as a practice opportunity after instruction of the concept through Activity 6.3 ("To Algorithm or Not to Algorithm").

Materials: This routine does not require any materials.

Directions: 1. Pose a few problems to students.

2. Have students discuss with a partner which problems are good candidates for solving with an algorithm and which are not.

3. Have students explain their decisions. Be sure to avoid implying that any problem should or must be solved with an algorithm.

That One		
559 – 376	519 – 304	856 – 448

TEACHING TAKEAWAY

You can use any problem for this routine, including problems from the previous routine and problems throughout this book.

In this example, 559 – 376 is most likely the only problem that is best suited for the algorithm. Students might suggest that 519 – 304 can be solved by counting back 300 or by using the constant difference, finding the difference of 515 – 304. The last one might be considered a problem for the algorithm by some. Students might suggest that it can be thought of as 858 – 450 or it can be solved by counting up.

ACTIVITY 6.8

Name: "Over/Under"　　　　**Type:** Routine

About the Routine: Determining reasonableness when using standard algorithms is critically important. In this routine, students determine if a sum or difference will be over or under (more or less) a given number.

Materials: Identify a target number for comparison and prepare a few addition or subtraction expressions that would likely be solved with the standard algorithm.

Directions:　1. Share the over/under number.

2. Pose each expression.

3. Have students estimate the sum or difference of each problem.

4. Students share their ideas with partners, and then discuss their approaches to reasoning with the class.

5. After ideas are shared, the exact solution can be found and compared to the over/under number.

Over/Under 5,000		
3,559 + 776	2,089 + 1,737	4,379 + 647

Students should deem the first sum to be under 5,000 because 4,000 + 1,000 = 5,000 and the addends in this problem are less than both of those addends. The regrouping in this first problem may cause student errors. So, it is important to stress to students why their reasoning makes sense and how it can help them. The last problem may be more challenging but can be reasoned that 4,400 + 600 would be more than 5,000.

Over/Under 2,500		
2,870 – 719	3,060 – 389	8,422 – 4,378

Again, regrouping is needed for each of these problems and errors are likely to occur, so estimating the difference is important for determining reasonableness. In the first problem, 2,800 – 700 is less than 2,500 so the original problem must be as well. In the second, students might reason that 3,060 – 500 is over 2,500, so then this problem is because it is not taking away 500. Like the others, the last problem can be thought of in a variety of ways. For example, students might instead think about adding 2,500 to 4,378 to determine if more or less would be needed. Reasoning about a missing addend is sound but may lead to confusion about the difference being more or less than the target.

ACTIVITY 6.9

Name: All Lined Up
(Addition or Subtraction)

Type: Game

About the Game: *All Lined Up* is a game of strategy and luck that gives students an opportunity to practice addition and subtraction with (or without) the standard algorithm.

Materials: *All Lined Up* game board, a collection of addition or subtraction problems, recording sheet

Directions:
1. Players take turns pulling an addition card and finding the sum.

2. A player records the sum in one of their six boxes.

3. On subsequent turns, the student must record the sum in a box as it relates to the other sums. In other words, the sums have to be recorded in order from least to greatest.

4. If a player can't place their sum, the player loses their turn.

5. The first player to fill all six boxes in order from least to greatest wins.

For example, a student pulled 1,477 + 4,558 and found the sum of 6,035. He recorded it in the third box. On his second turn, he found the sum of 9,081. On his third turn, he found a sum of 3,457. If he would pick 3,679 + 1,589 on his next turn, he would lose his turn because there is no space to place the sum of 5,268.

All Lined Up

Directions: Pull a problem card. Find the sum or difference. Place the sum or difference in one of the boxes so that they are in order from least to greatest.

	3,457	6,035			9,081

RESOURCE(S) FOR THIS ACTIVITY

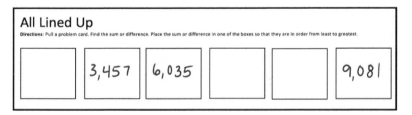

online resources ▸ This resource can be downloaded at **resources.corwin.com/FOF/addsubtractwholenumber**.

ACTIVITY 6.10

Name: The V Cover Up   **Type:** Game

About the Game: *The V Cover Up* is an opportunity to practice adding or subtracting. The numbers on the game board match addition and subtraction problem cards. The goal is to get an unusual connection of three counters or game pieces.

Materials: *V Cover Up* game board, counters, expression cards, calculators

Directions: 1. Players take turns pulling addition and subtraction cards and finding the sum or difference.

2. The player covers the sum or difference they find on the game board. Their opponent checks their accuracy first by doing the problem and then with a calculator.

3. If the sum is already taken, or the player adds incorrectly, the player loses their turn.

4. The first player to make a three-space V wins.

The following image shows how to make a three-space V. The V can be oriented in any way.

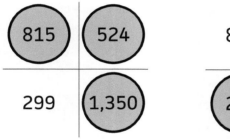

TEACHING TAKEAWAY

Consider adding an estimation component to games to develop the good math habit of expecting certain results in case mistakes are made when calculating.

RESOURCE(S) FOR THIS ACTIVITY

Expressions to use for the game include the following:

556 + 251	911 − 192	645 + 218	632 + 728	1,243 − 439	9,324 − 7,974
189 + 118	1,073 − 268	471 + 232	118 + 697	2,459 − 1,705	528 − 229
479 + 173	1,201 − 348	918 + 164	342 + 382	2,064 − 1,225	792 − 250
525 + 289	903 − 132	805 + 376	465 + 319	1,083 − 1,225	801 − 198
542 + 363	824 − 118	269 + 512	925 + 158	5,383 − 4,311	822 − 198

online resources This resource can be downloaded at **resources.corwin.com/FOF/addsubtractwholenumber**.

ACTIVITY 6.11

Name: A List of Ten   **Type:** Game

About the Game: In terms of procedural fluency, knowing when to use an algorithm is just as important as knowing how to use an algorithm. Yet students don't have frequent opportunities to consider when to use an algorithm. *A List of Ten* is a game for considering when an algorithm is useful and when it isn't. It is the perfect complement to instructional Activity 6.3 ("To Algorithm or Not to Algorithm").

Materials: addition or subtraction expression cards, *A List of Ten* game board

Directions: 1. Expression cards are shuffled and placed face down.

2. Players take turns selecting a card and determining if the expression is best solved with or without the algorithm. Note that if a player can tell their opponent why an expression is better solved without an algorithm, they can steal the card from their opponent.

3. The player records the equation in the appropriate column.

4. The first player to get a list of 10 wins.

5. After the game, both players solve each problem on their game board.

RESOURCE(S) FOR THIS ACTIVITY

A List of Ten

Directions: Players take turns flipping over cards and deciding if the problem is best solved with or without the standard algorithm. Players can steal problem cards to put in the algorithm list if they can explain how a different strategy could be used to solve the problem.

Problems that can be solved WITHOUT the STANDARD ALGORITHM	Problems that are best solved WITH the STANDARD ALGORITHM
1.	1.
2.	2.
3.	3.
4.	4.
5.	5.
6.	6.
7.	7.
8.	8.
9.	9.
10.	10.

online resources — Expression cards and this recording sheet can be downloaded at **resources.corwin.com/FOF/addsubtractwholenumber**.

ACTIVITY 6.12

Name: Add-tzee   **Type:** Game

About the Game: *Add-tzee* (or *Sub-tzee*) is a take on the classic dice game, *Yahtzee*. It is an engaging way to practice addition or subtraction with (or without) the standard algorithm. *Add-tzee* can be modified in all sorts of ways. You can change the number of digits in each addend. If so, you will need to change the conditions on the game board accordingly. For example, if students are making two-digit addends, the sixth condition would be "Sum is less than 50" instead of "Sum is less than 500." *Sub-tzee* is the subtraction version of the same game.

Materials: 10-sided dice, four decks of digit cards (0–9), or playing cards (queens = 0, aces = 1, kings and jacks removed); *Add-tzee* game board

Directions:

1. Players deal themselves three digit cards to make a number and three more digit cards to make another number.

2. The players add the two numbers using the standard algorithm or another strategy.

3. After finding the sum, the players use the problem (with the sum) to satisfy one of the conditions on the game board by recording it in the corresponding space.

4. After each turn, the player must choose one of the places on the game board for the sum they found or take a 0 for that condition.

5. After 11 turns, the players add their scores with the highest score winning.

Note that there are two chance spaces on the game board. In these spaces, the sum is the point value for the condition.

RESOURCE(S) FOR THIS ACTIVITY

Add-tzee

Directions: Make an addition problem with digit cards. Find the sum. Choose a space to record your sum. You only have 11 turns.

Player 1			Player 2		
	Points	My problem		Points	My Problem
Even Sum	100		Even Sum	100	
Odd Sum	100		Odd Sum	100	
Sum with a 5 in it	100		Sum with a 5 in it	100	
Sum with a 3 in it	100		Sum with a 3 in it	100	
Sum has two digits that are the same	500		Sum has two digits that are the same	500	
Sum is greater than 500	100		Sum is greater than 500	100	
Sum is less than 500	100		Sum is less than 500	100	
Sum between 500 and 750	200		Sum between 500 and 750	200	
Chance (Sum is your score)			Chance (Sum is your score)		
Chance (Sum is your score)			Chance (Sum is your score)		
Sum is 1,000	1,000		Sum is 1,000	1,000	
Total score			Total score		

online resources ⟶ Digit cards and this recording sheet can be downloaded at **resources.corwin.com/FOF/ addsubtractwholenumber**.

ACTIVITY 6.13

Name: The Connects   **Type:** Game

About the Game: *The Connects* is an engaging way to practice addition or subtraction. It is played similarly to the classic board game, *Boggle*, as students find sums and differences through connected digits.

Materials: *The Connects* game board; digit cards (0–9), playing cards (queens = 0, aces = 1, kings and jacks removed), or addition/subtraction cards; paper for recording work

Directions: 1. Players make a game board by randomly placing digits in each grid as shown in the example.

2. Players use digit cards to make an addition or subtraction problem. As an alternative, you can provide cards with addition or subtraction problems on them.

3. Both players solve the problem.

4. Players look for the sum or difference on the game board they made by finding adjacent digits.

5. Players get 1 point for each example they find. The first player to reach a set goal (e.g., 10 points) or the most points after five problems wins.

For example, two players made the problem 487 – 466, finding a difference of 21. Player 1 found 21 two times, earning 2 points as shown. Player 2 found 21 three times, earning 3 points.

Player 1   Player 2

The Connects   ## The Connects

7	5	4	9	8
4	2	3	8	3
1	2	9	6	4
5	5	9	3	2
6	1	1	3	7

1	3	6	4	8
9	1	2	3	8
5	6	4	4	1
3	8	7	2	1
3	7	9	4	8

online resources — Digit cards, addition or subtraction cards, and this game board can be downloaded at **resources.corwin.com/FOF/addsubtractwholenumber**.

ACTIVITY 6.14

Name: Algorithm Problem Sort   **Type:** Center

About the Center: This center challenges students to think about how best to solve an addition or subtraction problem. Students can use the downloadable recording sheet or write their ideas in their math journals. Either option is useful for holding students accountable during the independent work and for assessing. You can use any downloadable problem cards from any module in this book or create your own. You can extend the center by asking students to create their own examples of problems best solved with or without the algorithm. Or you can ask students to identify a problem from each column and tell why they placed the problem in that column.

Materials: addition or subtraction problem cards, Algorithm Problem Sort recording sheet

Directions: 1. Students select a problem card.

2. Students record the problem in the "Problems That Are Best Solved With the Standard Algorithm" or "Problems That Can Be Solved Without the Standard Algorithm" column.

3. Then students record the sum or difference (dependent upon the operations they are working with).

RESOURCE(S) FOR THIS ACTIVITY

Algorithm Problem Sort

Directions: Select a problem card. Decide if the problem is best solved with the standard algorithm or not and record the problem in the corresponding column. Then, solve the problem.

Problems that can be solved WITHOUT the STANDARD ALGORITHM	Problems that are best solved WITH the STANDARD ALGORITHM
1.	1.
2.	2.
3.	3.
4.	4.
5.	5.
6.	6.
7.	7.
8.	8.
9.	9.
10.	10.

online resources ► Problem cards and this recording sheet can be downloaded at **resources.corwin.com/FOF/addsubtractwholenumber**.

ACTIVITY 6.15

Name: Missing Numbers With Addition and Subtraction Algorithms   **Type:** Center

About the Center: This activity helps students practice finding and correcting additions and subtraction errors. This center can be complemented with a writing component. For example, after students complete a Missing Numbers card, they can be expected to write about how they found the missing digit or to justify how they know their solution is correct.

$$
\begin{array}{r}
2\ ? \\
+\ ?\ 7 \\
\hline
1\ 0\ 6
\end{array}
$$

Materials: prepared Missing Number problem cards (see note below directions)

Directions: 1. Students select a Missing Number problem card.

2. Students work to find the Missing Number(s) in the algorithm.

To make Missing Number problem cards, create a problem and then simply change out one or more digits with a question mark (?). The template provided here is for two-digit addends with regrouping. Additional templates are available for download. Those templates feature two-, three-, and four-digit addition with and without regrouping. There are also templates for subtraction.

RESOURCE(S) FOR THIS ACTIVITY

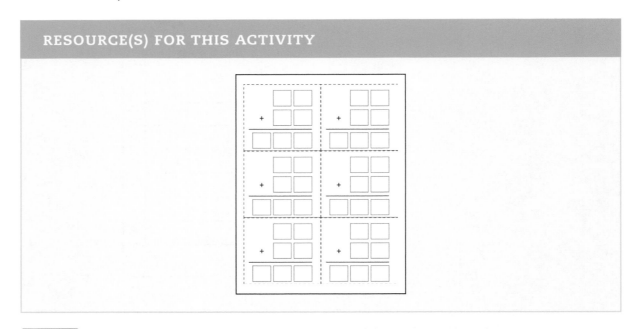

online resources — This resource can be downloaded at **resources.corwin.com/FOF/addsubtractwholenumber**.

PUTTING IT ALL TOGETHER
Developing Fluency

FLUENCY IS . . .

How might you finish a sentence that begins "Fluency is . . ."? One way is "using procedures efficiently, flexibly, and accurately." Another option is "important." Or maybe fluency is "an equity issue." All of these are true statements. This section is the capstone of this book on fluency with addition and subtraction of whole numbers. If students learn a strategy in isolation and never get to practice choosing when to use it, they will not become truly fluent. Part 3 focuses on learning to *choose* strategies. The following lists reflect subsets of the Seven Significant Strategies.

ADDITION "MUST KNOW" STRATEGIES	SUBTRACTION "MUST KNOW" STRATEGIES
• Count On	• Count Back
• Make Tens (or Hundreds, etc.)	• Think Addition (Count Up)
• Compensation	• Compensation
• Partial Sums	• Partial Differences

Once students know more than one strategy, they need opportunities to practice choosing strategies. In other words, you do not want to wait until they have learned all strategies and the standard algorithms before they begin choosing from among the strategies they know. For example, if you are teaching subtraction with Compensation, you have likely taught Count Back or Think Addition. So, it is time to use a Part 3 activity to help students decide *when* they will use each strategy. Then, add a new strategy to students' repertoire and return again to activities that focus on choosing a strategy. This iterative process continues through the teaching of standard algorithms, as students continue to accumulate methods for adding and subtracting whole numbers. Along the way, it is important that students also learn that sometimes there is more than one good way to solve a problem, and other times, one way really stands out from the others.

CHOICE

Choosing strategies is at the heart of fluency. After a strategy is learned, it should always be an option for consideration. Too often students feel like when they have moved on to a new strategy, they are supposed to use only the new one, as though it is more sophisticated or preferred by their teacher. But the strategies are additive—they form a collection from which students can select in order to solve the problem at hand.

Once students know how and why a strategy works, they need to figure out when it makes sense to use the strategy. That is when you need questions such as these:

● When do you/might you use a Counting Up strategy for subtraction?

● When do you/might you use a Make Tens strategy for addition?

● When do you/might you use Partial Sums? Partial Differences?

● When do you/might you use Compensation for addition? Subtraction?

● When do you/might you use a standard algorithm?

- When do you/might you not use _____ strategy/algorithm?
- Which strategies do you think of first when you see a problem?
- Which strategies do you choose only after other options don't work?
- Which strategies do you avoid?

The first six prompts can be mapped to the Part 2 modules (and asked during instruction on those strategies, as well as during mixed practice). As students are exploring the Make Tens strategy, for example, include regular questioning about when it is a good fit and when it is not. The full set of questions is essential to the development of fluency. Activities are woven throughout the modules to help identify when a strategy works best and when it doesn't. However, those activities don't necessarily bring other strategies into consideration. Part 3 focuses on this notion of putting it all together, which includes attending to metacognition.

METACOGNITION

As students become more proficient with the strategies they have learned and when to use them, they make decisions as to what they will do for a given problem. Taking time up front to make a good choice can save time in the enactment of a not-efficient strategy. We can help students with this reasoning by sharing a metacognitive process. This could be a bulletin board or a card taped to students' desks. We can remind students that as we work, we make good choices about the methods we use. This is *flexibility* in action.

METACOGNITIVE PROCESS FOR SELECTING A STRATEGY

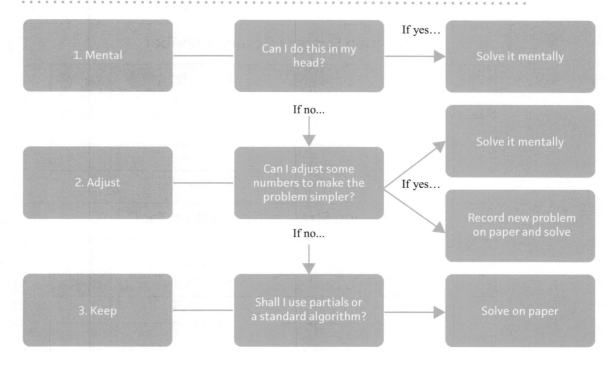

ASSESSING FLUENCY

Traditionally, fluency assessment has focused on speed and accuracy. While accuracy does matter, it is only one-third of what it means to be fluent. As you assess fluency, you want to intentionally look for each of the three fluency components and the six Fluency Actions. Flexibility and efficiency can be observed as students engage in meaningful activities. There is no need to stop and give a test.

See Chapter 7 (pp. 154–175) of *Figuring Out Fluency* for more information about assessing fluency.

OBSERVATION TOOLS

Observation tools can help us focus on the "neglected" components of fluency and serve as a way to communicate with students and their parents about what real fluency looks like. Three examples are shared here.

Student: _____   Date: _____

Problem(s): _____

Fluency Actions Checklist

Procedural Fluency Actions	Evident?			Comments
1. Selects appropriate strategy	Yes	No	Not Observed	
2. Solves in a reasonable amount of time	Yes	No	Not Observed	
3. Trades out or adapts a strategy	Yes	No	Not Observed	
4. Applies strategy to a new problem type	Yes	No	Not Observed	
5. Completes steps correctly	Yes	No	Not Observed	
6. Gets correct answer	Yes	No	Not Observed	

Comments:

Addition Strategy Observation Tool

Student Name	Addition Strategies				Algorithm
	Count On	Make Tens	Compensation	Partial Sums	

Subtraction Strategy Observation Tool

Student Name	Subtraction Strategies				Algorithm
	Count Back	Think Addition	Compensation	Partial Differences	

 These resources can be downloaded at **resources.corwin.com/FOF/ addsubtractwholenumber**.

GRADING ASSIGNMENTS AND ASSESSMENTS

All of your efforts to teach strategies and to teach students to choose efficient strategies must be continued through assessments. Too often tests are graded for accuracy only. Instead, provide a fluency score using a rubric, such as the one that follows.

FOUR-POINT FLUENCY RUBRIC

BEGINNING 1	DEVELOPING 2	EMERGING 3	ACCOMPLISHED 4
Knows one algorithm or strategy but continues to get stuck or make errors.	Demonstrates efficiency and accuracy with at least one strategy/ algorithm but does not stop to think if there is a more efficient possibility.	Demonstrates efficiency and accuracy with several strategies/ algorithms, and sometimes selects an efficient strategy, although still figuring out when to use and not use a strategy.	Demonstrates efficiency and accuracy with several strategies/algorithms and is adept at matching problems with efficient strategies (knowing when to use each and when not to).

With an eye on fluency and how to assess it, select fluency activities from Part 3 based on your students' needs and what type of activity you are seeking.

FLUENCY ACTIVITIES

The nine activities in this section focus on all components of fluency, providing students with the opportunity to practice choosing an appropriate strategy, enact that strategy, and reflect on the efficiency of the strategies selected.

ACTIVITY F.1

Name: "Strategize First Steps"   **Type:** Routine

About the Routine: This routine involves sharing how to *start* a problem. It is at this first step that students are selecting a strategy. In its quickest version, that is the only step that is ever done. Simply ask, "Which step first and why?" A second option begins the same way but after students have shared ideas for first steps, they get to choose which first step they like and finish the problem. Then, answers can be shared and students can reflect on which first step turned out to be a good one (and why).

Materials: list of three or four problems on the same topic, but that lend to different reasoning strategies

(Continued)

(Continued)

Directions: This routine involves showing a series of problems, one at a time, like a Number Talk (Parrish, 2014). But it differs in the fact that the tasks you selected *do not* lend to the same strategy. Here is the routine process:

1. Ask students to mentally determine their first step (only) and signal when they're ready (since it is only the first step, they only need a few seconds).

2. Record first-step ideas by creating a list on the board.

3. Discuss which first steps seem reasonable (or not).

4. Repeat with two to four more problems, referring to the list created from the first problem and adding to the list if/when new strategies are shared.

5. Conclude the series with a discussion: When will you use _____ strategy?

Possible problem sets for this routine include the following:

TWO-DIGIT ADDITION	TWO-DIGIT SUBTRACTION
59 + 18 =	29 – 12 =
35 + 63 =	68 – 59 =
52 + 42 =	71 – 35 =
27 + 49 =	86 – 57 =
67 + 23 =	93 – 18 =
THREE-DIGIT ADDITION	**THREE-DIGIT SUBTRACTION**
185 + 415 =	550 – 125 =
490 + 535 =	658 – 639 =
258 + 347 =	606 – 597 =
315 + 575 =	990 – 125 =
207 + 465 =	621 – 571 =

Let's say you were using the list for two-digit subtraction. Here are some examples of the first steps you might hear for the first problem, 29 – 12:

"Jump down 10."

"Think of the 29 as a 30."

"Subtract 2."

"Count back 12."

You can layer in strategy names at this point. For example, label the first idea as Counting Back, the second as Compensation, and so on. Then, by consistent use of the language, students should begin to say, "I used Compensation and ..." For each problem, some of the same strategies will be named again, and new ideas might be added (e.g., someone might add, "Count up from 59"). If an idea doesn't come up, you can ask about it directly or just move to the next problem. Be mindful not to imply that it is the preferred approach. As noted earlier, if students are going to solve the problem, allow them to choose from the ideas that were first stated. They can later share if they stayed with their original first step or switched out to one of the ideas from their classmates.

ACTIVITY F.2

Name: "M-A-K-E a Decision"　　　　**Type:** Routine

About the Routine: Mental-Adjust-Keep-Expressions is a routine that, like other routines, can function for assessment purposes. Project for students an illustration of the metacognitive process, like the one discussed earlier in the Part 3 overview. If a problem can be solved mentally, there is no need to use a written method such as a standard algorithm. Students tend to dive in without stopping to think if they can solve a problem mentally. There are two ways to use the tasks in this routine. One is to show one problem at a time, each time asking, "Which way will you solve it?" Or you can show the full set and ask, "Which ones might you solve mentally? Adjust and solve? Keep as-is and solve?" The former is used below.

Materials: Prepare a set of three to six expressions.

Directions:

1. Explain that you are going to display a problem. Students are not to solve it but simply "M-A-K-E a Decision: Mental, Adjust and solve, or Keep and solve on paper?"

2. Display the first problem and give students about 10 seconds to decide.

3. Use a cue to have students share their choice (one finger = mental, two fingers = adjust, three fingers = keep and solve on paper).

4. Ask a student who picked each decision to share why (and how).

5. Repeat step 3, giving students a chance to change their minds.

6. Repeat for the next problem.

7. At the end of the set, ask, "What do you 'see' in a problem that leads to you doing it mentally? Adjusting? Keep and use paper?"

Possible problem sets to use with this routine include the following:

TWO-DIGIT ADDITION		TWO-DIGIT SUBTRACTION	
31 + 18	38 + 48	57 − 17	32 − 19
68 + 55	30 + 41	68 − 52	83 − 74
17 + 46	49 + 49	94 − 76	67 − 49

THREE-DIGIT ADDITION		THREE-DIGIT SUBTRACTION	
301 + 180	135 + 465	357 − 217	522 − 379
648 + 155	369 + 401	508 − 497	803 − 299
475 + 276	388 + 710	733 − 108	708 − 409

FOUR-DIGIT ADDITION		FOUR-DIGIT SUBTRACTION	
5,900 + 2,136	5,299 + 4,672	6,008 − 3,999	5,217 − 1,884
3,450 + 3,549	5,816 + 9,013	5,340 − 5,307	9,034 − 7,955
5,600 + 3,089	8,130 + 8,413	6,457 − 4,873	4,375 − 2,975

ACTIVITY F.3

Name: "Share–Share–Compare"   **Type:** Routine

About the Routine: This routine can also be a longer classroom activity, depending on how many problems students are asked to solve. Each person first solves problems independently, then has the chance to have a one-on-one with a peer to compare their thinking on the same problem.

Materials: Prepare a list of three to five problems that lend to being solved different ways.

Directions: 1. Students work independently to solve the full set of problems.

2. Students write if they solved it mentally by naming the strategy they used. If they solved it by writing, they do not need to name a strategy.

3. Once complete, everyone stands up with their page of worked problems.

4. Students find a partner who is *not* at their table. When they find a partner, they high-five each other and begin Share–Share–Compare for the first problem:

- Share: Partner 1 **shares** their method.
- Share: Partner 2 **shares** their method.
- Compare: Partners discuss how their methods **compared**:

If their methods are different, they compare the two, discussing which one worked the best or if both worked well.

If their methods are the same, they think of an alternative method and again discuss which method(s) worked well.

After the exchange, partners thank each other, raise their hands to indicate they are in search of a new partner, find another partner, and repeat the process of Share–Share–Compare for problem 2 (or any problem they haven't yet discussed).

Possible problem sets for this routine include the following:

ADDITION WITH TWO-DIGIT NUMBERS	SUBTRACTION WITH TWO-DIGIT NUMBERS
78 + 59	48 – 29
37 + 65	83 – 24
34 + 47 + 26	56 – 47
98 + 67	61 – 19

MIXED PROBLEM SET: TWO-DIGIT NUMBERS	MIXED PROBLEM SET: MULTIDIGIT NUMBERS
28 + 27	78 + 57
52 + 49	345 + 765
81 – 74	108 – 74
83 – 17	640 – 675
53 + 95	930 + 595
78 – 37	3,009 – 1,950

ACTIVITY F.4

Name: Strategy Spin   **Type:** Game

About the Game: This game can be played in many ways. You can have spinners that focus on metacognition (mental, adjust, keep; see metacognition visual), you can pick the strategies students know, or you can have the options "Standard Algorithm" and "Not Standard Algorithm." There are many online spinner tools, such as Wheel Decide (https://wheeldecide.com/), which allow you to enter the categories you want and actually spin virtually. This game can be played with two to four players.

Materials: strategy spinner (one per group) and expression cards

Directions:
1. Players take turns spinning the strategy spinner.

2. Once the spinner lands on a strategy, the player looks through the expression bank to find a problem they want to solve using that strategy.

3. The player tells how to solve the selected problem using that strategy. Opponents check solutions using a Hundred Chart, number line, or calculator. If correct, the player claims that expression card.

4. Repeat steps 2 and 3 three times for four players, four times for three players, and five times for two players.

5. Together the group looks at the remaining expressions and labels which strategy they think is a good fit for each.

RESOURCE(S) FOR THIS ACTIVITY

54 – 28	73 – 59
93 – 38	48 – 23
74 – 25	32 – 15
85 – 56	57 – 9

554 – 428	773 – 159
800 – 380	408 – 393
704 – 235	325 – 150
852 – 506	507 – 249

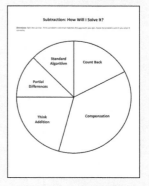

online resources   These resources can be downloaded at **resources.corwin.com/FOF/addsubtractwholenumber**.

ACTIVITY F.5

Name: Just Right   **Type:** Game

About the Game: This game board can be adapted to incorporate the strategies students have learned. Earlier in the year, it may have three options; later in the year, it may have five options. Students may be tempted to use inefficient strategies in order to get four in a row. To counter this, require students to record the equations and the strategy they used.

Materials: expression cards (mixed strategies), *Just Right* game board, and two-sided counters

Directions: 1. Players take turns flipping cards.

2. Player selects a "just right" strategy, and solves it thinking aloud or on paper.

3. Opponents confirm accuracy with calculators.

4. Having correctly solved the problem, the player places a marker on the strategy they used on the *Just Right* game board.

5. The first player to place four markers in a row on the game board wins.

For example, Sydney draws 68 + 28. She says, "My *Just Right* strategy is Compensation. I think 70 + 30 equals 100, but that is 4 too many, so I subtract 4 to equal 96." Her opponent, Annie, confirms that she is correct. Sydney covers her choice of a Compensation square.

RESOURCE(S) FOR THIS ACTIVITY

Just Right: Addition Board

Directions: Flip over a problem card. Decide which strategy is "just right" for the problem. Place a marker on the strategy. Be the first to get four markers in a row (horizontally, vertically, or diagonally).

Compensation	Count On	Make Tens (or Hundreds)	Standard Algorithm	Partial Sums
Partial Sums	Make Tens (or Hundreds)	Compensation	Count On	Compensation
Make Tens (or Hundreds)	Standard Algorithm	Count On	Compensation	Partial Sums
Partial Sums	Make Tens (or Hundreds)	Compensation	Standard Algorithm	Make Tens (or Hundreds)
Compensation	Partial Sums	Count On	Standard Algorithm	Partial Sums

Just Right: Subtraction Board

Directions: Flip over a problem card. Decide which strategy is "just right" for the problem. Place a marker on the strategy. Be the first to get four markers in a row (horizontally, vertically, or diagonally).

Compensation	Count Back	Think Addition	Standard Algorithm	Partial Differences
Partial Differences	Think Addition	Compensation	Count Back	Compensation
Think Addition	Standard Algorithm	Compensation	Standard Algorithm	Partial Differences
Standard Algorithm	Think Addition	Count Back	Compensation	Think Addition
Compensation	Think Addition	Count Back	Standard Algorithm	Partial Differences

online resources Game cards and game boards can be downloaded at **resources.corwin.com/FOF/addsubtractwholenumber**.

ACTIVITY F.6

Name: *Strategories*   **Type:** *Game*

About the Game: This game is an excellent opportunity for practice or assessment once a variety of strategies are learned. Students generate three to six examples of problems that lend to using that strategy, such as 29 + 7, 58 + 25, or 319 + 348 (depending on grade level). The directions describe this as a small group activity, but it can be modified to a center. An alternative to this game is to just focus on one strategy (e.g., Make Tens).

Materials: *Strategies* game card (one per student)

Directions:
1. Each player works independently to generate a problem for which they would use that strategy (alternatively, students can work with a partner to discuss problems that would fit in each strategy).

2. After players have completed their *Strategies* game card (i.e., has one example expression in each strategy), place students in groups of three.

3. On a player's turn, they ask one of the other group members to share the problem on their *Strategies* card for _____ strategy. If the player explains the problem using that strategy, they score 5 points. If not, the third player gets a chance to "steal" by explaining the problem using that strategy. If the third player cannot, the author of the problem must explain using that strategy. If they cannot, they lose 10 points.

4. Play continues until all strategies have been solved, or students have played three rounds. The high score wins!

5. To facilitate discussion after play, ask questions such as these: What do you notice about the problems in _____ strategy? When is this strategy useful?

RESOURCE(S) FOR THIS ACTIVITY

Strategies: Subtraction

Strategy	My Problem
Count Back	
Think Addition	
Compensation	
Partial Differences	

Strategies: Addition

Strategy	My Problem
Count On	
Make Tens	
Compensation	
Partial Sums	

online resources ☝ These resources can be downloaded at **resources.corwin.com/FOF/addsubtractwholenumber**.

ACTIVITY F.7

Name: Make 100   **Type:** Game

About the Game: As students encounter different two-digit addends, they will find expressions that lend to different strategies. That makes this a good game for observing what strategies students are commonly choosing to use (and whether they are using a variety of strategies). The game can be played as a center in which students play to get their personal best score.

Materials: two sets of digit cards (0–9) or half a deck of playing cards (queens = 0, aces = 1, kings and jacks removed), *Make 100* game board

Directions:
1. Each player is dealt six cards. Note that cards are shuffled before each round.

2. Each player uses four of the six cards to make 2 two-digit addends with a sum as close to 100 as possible.

3. The player records their equation and shows how they found the sum.

4. Players record how far away they are from 100.

5. After five rounds, each player adds the distance from 100 from each round for a score.

6. The player with the lower score wins.

For example, Oscar pulls 5, 3, 4, 7, 2, and 1. He makes 43 + 57. He scores 0 points for the first round.

RESOURCE(S) FOR THIS ACTIVITY

Make 100

Directions: Deal six cards. Use four cards to make two addends with a sum as close to 100 as possible. Find the sum and show how you added. Record how far from 100 you are for each round.

Round	My Cards	My Addition Problem	How Far from 100?
1			
2			
3			
4			
5			

ACTIVITY F.8

Name: A-MAZE-ing Race   **Type:** Game

About the Game: This game is not about speed! Putting time pressure on students works against fluency, as the stress can block good reasoning. The purpose of this game is to practice selecting and using strategies that are a good fit for the numbers in the problem. It can be adapted for any addition or subtraction problem sets. You can also use it as a center in which students highlight their path, record the problems, find the solutions, and show their strategy.

Materials: *A-MAZE-ing Race* game board (one per pair), two-sided counters, calculators

Directions:
1. Players both put their marker on Start.

2. Players take turns selecting an unoccupied square that shares a border with their current position.

3. Players talk aloud to say the answer and explain how they solved the equation. An optional sentence frame to use is, "The answer is __. I used __ strategy to solve it. I __, then I __."

4. Opponents confirm accuracy with calculators. If correct, the player moves to the new square.

5. Note that the dark lines cannot be crossed.

6. The winner is the first to reach the finish.

RESOURCE(S) FOR THIS ACTIVITY

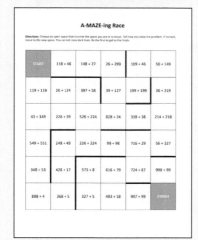

online resources — These resources can be downloaded at **resources.corwin.com/FOF/addsubtractwholenumber**.

ACTIVITY F.9

Name: Strategy Problem Sort　　　　　　　　　　**Type:** Center

About the Center: Just because a problem can be solved with a given strategy does not mean it is a good fit. It is a good fit when it is the most appropriate option from a student's set of known strategies. (See the Part 1 discussion of appropriate strategies.) You can extend the activity by having students go through the "Does Not Fit the Strategy" category and identify which strategy would work well for that problem.

Materials: Strategy Problem Sort cards or a set of 12–20 mixed problems (some that fit the intended strategy and some that do not), Strategy Problem Sort placemat

Directions:　　1. Students flip over a problem card.

　　　　　　　　2. Students determine if the problem fits the strategy or doesn't fit the strategy.

　　　　　　　　3. Students then solve the problem.

To create assessment artifacts, you can take a picture of a student's completed sort. Or, you can ask students to provide written responses to questions like these:

I placed _____ in the "Fits the Strategy" side because …

I placed _____ in the "Does Not Fit the Strategy" side because …

RESOURCE(S) FOR THIS ACTIVITY

Strategy Sort Placemat

Strategy: _____

Fits the Strategy	Doesn't Fit the Strategy

399 + 447	516 + 628
601 + 99	344 + 744
119 + 350	434 + 697
610 + 529	535 + 395
952 + 863	374 + 259

601 − 399	744 − 516
447 − 99	628 − 344
610 − 119	697 − 535
529 − 350	434 − 395
990 − 99	732 − 271

online resources ⬉ These resources can be downloaded at **resources.corwin.com/FOF/addsubtractwholenumber**.

Appendix
Tables of Activities

Figuring out fluency is a journey. Fluency with whole number addition and subtraction is absolutely essential for life and for future mathematics. Each and every child must have access and ample opportunities to develop their understanding and use of reasoning strategies. It is critical to remember these points:

- Fluency needs to be a daily part of mathematics instruction.

- There are no shortcuts or quick fixes to developing fluency.

- Fluency requires instruction *and* ongoing reinforcement.

- Different students require different types and quantities of experiences to develop fluency.

- While strategy choice is about the individual student, every student must learn and practice significant strategies so that they *can* choose to use them.

- Fluency practice must not be stressful. Stress complicates thinking.

- Fluency is more than accuracy; you must assess the other components.

This book is packed with activities for instruction, practice, and assessment to support the work that you do and to supplement the resources you use. The following pages provide a listing of all of the activities in this book. These tables can help you achieve the following:

- Jump between strategies, as you may not teach them sequentially.

- Locate prompts for teaching each strategy.

- Identify a specific type of activity to incorporate into your fluency instruction.

- Identify activities for specific strategies that you need to reteach, reinforce, or assess.

- Take notes about revisiting an activity later in the year.

- Take notes about modifying an activity for use with another strategy.

- Take notes about how you might leverage the activity in future years.

- Identify an activity that is particularly useful for assessment.

MODULE 1: COUNT ON/COUNT BACK ACTIVITIES				
NO.	**PAGE**	**TYPE**	**NAME**	**NOTES**
1.1	22	T	Connecting Representations When Counting On (Count On)	
1.2	23	T	Connecting Representations When Counting Back (Count Back)	
1.3	23	T	Beaded Number Lines	
1.4	25	T	Number Bonds for Count On/Count Back in Chunks	
1.5	25	T	Prompts for Teaching Count On/Count Back	
1.6	29	R	"Or You Could" (renaming chunks)	
1.7	30	R	"The Count" (skip-counting by chunks)	
1.8	31	R	"Strategize First Jumps"	
1.9	32	G	*Count On Bingo*	
1.10	33	G	*Pick Your Jumps*	
1.11	34	G	*Make It Close*	
1.12	35	C	Find the Equation	
1.13	36	C	Same But Different (comparing jumps of different sizes)	
1.14	37	C	The Largest Sum, The Smallest Sum	

T (Teaching) • R (Routine) • G (Game) • C (Center/Independent)

MODULE 2: MAKE TENS ACTIVITIES				
NO.	PAGE	TYPE	NAME	NOTES
2.1	40	T	Connecting Trains (linking cubes for making 10)	
2.2	41	T	Expression Match	
2.3	41	T	Two-Card Equations (using ten-frames)	
2.4	42	T	Same and Different (comparing expressions and Make Tens adjustments)	
2.5	43	T	Prompts for Teaching Make Tens	
2.6	46	R	"Paired Quick Looks"	
2.7	47	R	"Say It As a Make Tens" (renaming expressions)	
2.8	48	R	"This Is Like ___ Because" (using Make Tens facts)	
2.9	49	G	*Make It, Take It*	
2.10	50	G	*Winning Streak*	
2.11	51	G	*Give Some to Make Ten*	
2.12	52	C	Making Make Tens (or Hundreds)	
2.13	53	C	Combinations Solitaire	
2.14	55	C	Rewrite It	
2.15	56	C	Changing Addends, Changing Sums	

T (Teaching) • R (Routine) • G (Game) • C (Center/Independent)

			MODULE 3: PARTIAL SUMS AND DIFFERENCES ACTIVITIES	
NO.	**PAGE**	**TYPE**	**NAME**	**NOTES**
3.1	61	T	Bag of Blocks (base-10 blocks)	
3.2	62	T	Partial Sums With Expander Cards	
3.3	63	T	Making Connections (between representations)	
3.4	63	T	The Missing Problem	
3.5	64	T	Prompts for Teaching Partial Sums and Differences	
3.6	68	R	"The Parts"	
3.7	70	R	"Complex Number Strings"	
3.8	71	R	"Too Much Taken?" (partial differences focus)	
3.9	72	G	*For Keeps*	
3.10	73	G	*Sum Duel*	
3.11	74	G	*100 or 0*	
3.12	75	G	*Partial Concentration*	
3.13	76	C	Partial Sums With Ten-Frames and Place Value Disks	
3.14	78	C	Target 1,000	

T (Teaching) • R (Routine) • G (Game) • C (Center/Independent)

			MODULE 4: COMPENSATION ACTIVITIES	
NO.	**PAGE**	**TYPE**	**NAME**	**NOTES**
4.1	83	T	Establishing Compensation Through Length (linking cubes)	
4.2	84	T	The Jumps Have It (using Hundred Charts)	
4.3	85	T	Adjusting One or Both? (constant differences)	
4.4	86	T	Generalize and Justify	
4.5	86	T	Meter Stick Compensation (Constant Difference)	
4.6	87	T	Three for Me (three different ways to adjust)	
4.7	89	T	Prompts for Teaching Compensation	
4.8	92	R	"Or You Could ... " (restating expressions using Compensation)	
4.9	93	R	"Why Not?" (considering when to use Compensation)	
4.10	94	G	*Who's Adjusting?*	
4.11	95	G	*Compensation Concentration*	
4.12	96	G	*Compensation Race*	
4.13	97	C	Compensation Lane	
4.14	98	C	Create Compensations	
4.15	99	C	Prove It	
4.16	100	C	One and the Other	

T (Teaching) • R (Routine) • G (Game) • C (Center/Independent)

MODULE 5: THINK ADDITION ACTIVITIES				
NO.	**PAGE**	**TYPE**	**NAME**	**NOTES**
5.1	104	T	Start With, Get To (With Hundred Charts)	
5.2	105	T	Think Addition With Bar Diagrams	
5.3	105	T	Number Line Proofs	
5.4	106	T	What's Missing? (with triangle cards)	
5.5	106	T	What's the Temperature? (vertical number lines)	
5.6	107	T	Prompts for Teaching Think Addition	
5.7	110	R	"Two Lies and a Truth"	
5.8	111	R	"Jump in Chunks" (estimating differences)	
5.9	112	G	*The Smallest Difference*	
5.10	113	G	*Target 0 or Bust*	
5.11	114	G	*Think Addition Math Libs*	
5.12	115	C	Think Addition Blocks (base-10 blocks)	
5.13	116	C	Triangle Cards	
5.14	117	C	Guess and Check	
5.15	118	C	Sentence Strip Reverso	
5.16	119	C	Make the Difference	

T (Teaching) • R (Routine) • G (Game) • C (Center/Independent)

MODULE 6: STANDARD ALGORITHM ACTIVITIES				
NO.	**PAGE**	**TYPE**	**NAME**	**NOTES**
6.1	122	T	They ARE the Same! (connecting partials and algorithms)	
6.2	123	T	Connecting Partials and Algorithms (symbolically)	
6.3	124	T	To Algorithm or Not to Algorithm (deciding when to use an algorithm)	
6.4	124	T	Rethinking Subtraction With Zeros	
6.5	125	T	Prompts for Teaching Standard Algorithms	
6.6	129	R	"Between and About" (estimating)	
6.7	130	R	"That One" (choosing when to use the algorithm)	
6.8	131	R	"Over/Under" (estimating)	
6.9	132	G	*All Lined Up* (Addition or Subtraction)	
6.10	133	G	*The V Cover Up*	
6.11	134	G	*A List of Ten*	
6.12	135	C	*Add-tzee*	
6.13	136	C	*The Connects*	
6.14	137	C	Algorithm Problem Sort	
6.15	138	C	Missing Numbers With Addition and Subtraction Algorithms	

T (Teaching) • R (Routine) • G (Game) • C (Center/Independent)

PART 3: CHOOSING AND USING STRATEGIES				
NO.	PAGE	TYPE	NAME	NOTES
F.1	143	R	"Strategize First Steps"	
F.2	145	R	"M-A-K-E a Decision"	
F.3	146	R	"Share–Share–Compare"	
F.4	147	G	*Strategy Spin*	
F.5	148	G	*Just Right*	
F.6	149	G	*Strategories*	
F.7	150	G/C	*Make 100*	
F.8	151	G/C	*A-MAZE-ing Race*	
F.9	152	C	Strategy Problem Sort	

T (Teaching) • R (Routine) • G (Game) • C (Center/Independent)

References

Baroody, A. J., & Dowker, A. (Eds.). (2003). *Studies in mathematical thinking and learning. The development of arithmetic concepts and skills: Constructing adaptive expertise.* Lawrence Erlbaum Associates.

Baroody, A. J., Purpura, D. J., Eiland, M. D., Reid, E. E., & Paliwal, V. (2016). Does fostering reasoning strategies for relatively difficult basic combinations promote transfer by K–3 students? *Journal of Educational Psychology*, 108(4), 576–591. https://psycnet.apa.org/doi/10.1037/edu0000067

Bay-Williams, J., & Kling, G. (2019). *Math fact fluency: 60+ games and assessment tools to support learning and retention.* ASCD.

Boaler, J. (2015a). *What's math got to do with it? How teachers and parents can transform mathematics learning and inspire success.* Penguin Books.

Boaler, J. (2015b). *Memorizers are the lowest achievers and other Common Core math surprises.* https://hechingerreport.org/memorizers-are-the-lowest-achievers-and-other-common-core-math-surprises/

Brendefur, J., Strother, S., Thiede, K., & Appleton, S. (2015). Developing multiplication fact fluency. *Advances in Social Sciences Research Journal*, 2(8), 142–154. https://doi.org/10.14738/assrj.28.1396

Cheind, J., & Schneider, W. (2012). The brain's learning and control architecture. *Current Directions in Psychological Science*, 21(2), 78–84. https://www.jstor.org/stable/23213097?seq=1

"Explicit." (2021). *Merriam-Webster.com.* https://www.merriam-webster.com/dictionary/explicit

Fuson, K. C., & Beckmann, S. (2012–2013, Fall/Winter). Standard algorithms in the Common Core State Standards. *NCSM Journal*, 14–30.

Franke, M. L., Kazemi, E., & Turrou, A. C. (2018). *Choral counting and counting collections: Transforming the PreK–5 math classroom.* Stenhouse Publishers.

Jameson, M. M. (2013). Contextual factors related to math anxiety in second-grade children. *Journal of Experimental Education*, 82(4), 518–536. https://doi.org/10.1080/00220973.2013.813367

Jordan, N. C., Kaplan, D., Ramineni, C., & Locuniak, M. N. (2009). Early math matters: Kindergarten number competence and later mathematics outcomes. *Developmental Psychology*, 45(3), 850–867. https://doi.org/10.1037/a0014939

Kilpatrick, J., Swafford, J., & Findell, B. (Eds.). (2001). *Adding it up: Helping children learn mathematics.* National Academy Press. https://doi.org/10.17226/9822

Locuniak, M. N., & Jordan, N. C. (2008). Using kindergarten number sense to predict calculation fluency in second grade. *Journal of Learning Disabilities*, 41(5), 451–459. https://doi.org/10.1177/0022219408321126

National Center for Education Statistics (NCES). NAEP Report Card: 2019 NAEP Mathematics Assessment. https://www.nationsreportcard.gov/mathematics/nation/achievement/?grade=4

National Council of Teachers of Mathematics (NCTM). (2014). *Principles to actions: Ensuring mathematical success for all.* NCTM.

O'Connell, S., & SanGiovanni, J. (2015). *Mastering the basic math facts in addition and subtraction: Strategies, activities, and interventions to move students beyond memorization.* Heinemann.

Parrish, S. (2014). *Number talks: Helping children build mental math and computation strategies, Grades K–5.* MathSolutions.

Purpura, D. J., Baroody, A. J., Eiland, M. D., & Reid, E. E. (2016). Fostering first graders' reasoning strategies with basic sums: The value of guided instruction. *The Elementary School Journal, 117*(1), 72–100. https://doi.org/10.1086/687809

Ramirez, G., Shaw, S. T., & Maloney, E. A. (2018). Math anxiety: Past research, promising interventions, and a new interpretation framework. *Educational Psychologist, 53*(3), 145–164. https://doi.org/10.1080/00461520.2018.1447384

SanGiovanni, J. J. (2019). *Daily routines to jump-start math class: Elementary school.* Corwin.

Star, J. R. (2005). Reconceptualizing conceptual knowledge. *Journal for Research in Mathematics Education, 36*(5), 404–411. https://doi.org/10.2307/30034943

Index

A SAGE Publishing Company

CORWIN HAS ONE MISSION: to enhance education through intentional professional learning.

We build long-term relationships with our authors, educators, clients, and associations who partner with us to develop and continuously improve the best evidence-based practices that establish and support lifelong learning.

Supporting TEACHERS | Empowering STUDENTS

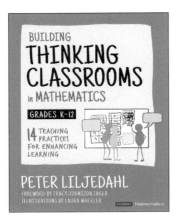

PETER LILJEDAHL

14 optimal practices for thinking that create an ideal setting for deep mathematics learning to occur

Grades K–12

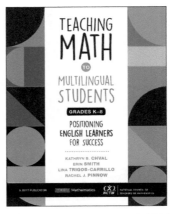

KATHRYN B. CHVAL, ERIN SMITH, LINA TRIGOS-CARRILLO, RACHEL J. PINNOW

Strengths-based approaches to support multilingual students' development in mathematics

Grades K–8

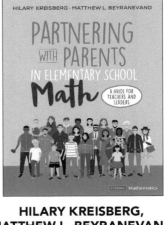

HILARY KREISBERG, MATTHEW L. BEYRANEVAND

Guidance on building productive relationships with families about math education

Grades K–5

BETH MCCORD KOBETT, FRANCIS (SKIP) FENNELL, KAREN S. KARP, DELISE ANDREWS, TRENDA KNIGHTEN, JEFF SHIH, DESIREE HARRISON, BARBARA ANN SWARTZ, SORSHA-MARIA T. MULROE

Detailed plans for helping elementary students experience deep mathematical learning

Grades K–1, 2–3, 4–5

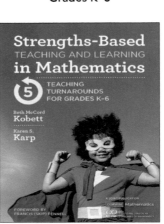

BETH MCCORD KOBETT, KAREN S. KARP

Your game plan for unlocking mathematics by focusing on students' strengths

Grades K–6

JOHN J. SANGIOVANNI, SUSIE KATT, KEVIN J. DYKEMA

Empowering students to embrace productive struggle to build essential skills for learning and living—both inside and outside the classroom

Grades K–12

To order, visit corwin.com/math

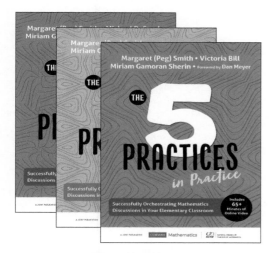
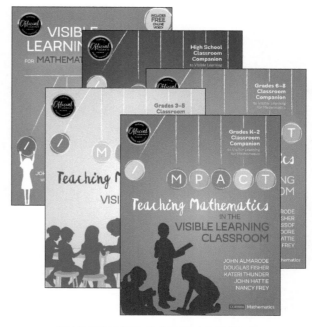

Supporting TEACHERS | Empowering STUDENTS

64 FREE grade-specific, standards-aligned, rich mathematical tasks for Grades K–8

At Corwin Mathematics, we believe ALL students should have the opportunity to be successful in math!

In addition to all of the practical tools designed explicitly for this book, please enjoy our gift of 64 FREE, grade-specific, standards-aligned, rich mathematical tasks downloadable at www.corwin.com/math/rich_tasks

rich tasks mathematics **This collection of rich tasks addresses the key content at each grade level. These tasks**

> > > Are designed with multiple entry points, making them accessible to all learners

> > > Invite students to wrestle with problems

> > > Contain multiple solution pathways

> > > Encourage use of multiple representations

> > > Promote mathematical discourse and student collaboration

Developed by Corwin Mathematics authors and other mathematics specialists, each task includes special guidance for teachers, including

> > > The mathematical topic or standards-aligned goal

> > > Directions for how to facilitate the task

> > > Language for making the mathematics visible

> > > How to make the mathematical task accessible to all learners

Finally, you'll find a tool to help you adapt ANY textbook or online task to better foster access and equity, align to rigorous mathematical goals, and use formative assessment to move learning forward.

CORWIN Mathematics